MISERY AND MISFORTUNE
SUDDEN DEATHS IN SUFFOLK
1851-1865

Geoffrey Robinson

Researched, written, and published by Geoffrey Robinson.

ISBN 978-0-9572292-5-9

All rights reserved. No part of this publication may be reproduced or transmitted in any form or by any means, electronic or mechanical, including photocopy, recording, or any information storage or retrieval system, without permission in writing from the publishers.

Printed in Great Britain by The Lavenham Press Limited.
First published in 2021
Copyright Geoffrey Robinson 2021

Front Cover: Wilby church and cottages (from an early 19th century engraving)
Back Cover: Worlingworth Mill (early 20th century sketch – unknown artist)

CONTENTS

Introduction	5
1851	7
1852	15
1853	19
1854	27
1855	35
1856	41
A Word About Coroners	54
1857	58
1858	67
1859	71
1860	80
1861	93
1862	105
1863	113
1864	129
1865	139
APPENDICES	List of Parishes
	List of Surnames

Introduction

By the time of the Great Exhibition of 1851, many transformative changes had begun to take effect in most areas of British society. It would take some time for those changes to filter down into Suffolk agricultural life. For example, it was not until the mid-1840s that railways and their hazards came to the county of Suffolk, twenty years after the opening of the Stockton-Darlington railway.

Agriculture, being the principal industry in the county, brought new hazards into the lives of the agricultural labourers in the form of complex machinery such as threshing machines. Working conditions for the agricultural worker were not improving; most labouring families remained abjectly poor as wages were held down by farmers who themselves struggled to make a living whilst the landowners continued to create and supplement their own wealth. The commutation of agricultural tithes put an additional financial burden on the farmers and it was only with the repeal of the Corn Laws that some relief was brought to the sector.

Throughout the 1850s, rural communities would suffer from a depletion of the working population as families migrated to the towns and cities where there was more work and, potentially, more steady work. Emigration also took away the workforce of tomorrow as young families looked for a brighter future overseas. Into this depressed agricultural economy, the old labourer soldiered on. There was still no-one to protect his rights as a worker nor was there sufficient education for his children to learn about life and the new hazards facing them in the real world.

Medical advances slowly appeared. Anaesthetic had been introduced into medical procedures by 1850 – this might have been a comfort to the poor soul who faced the amputation of a limb lost inside some devilish machine. But agricultural parishes saw less of these advances than the major towns and cities. Sudden and unexpected deaths still occurred in a great variety of ways. Diseases still took their toll of the poorer classes but, judging by the columns of the county newspapers, the incidence of sudden deaths and the need for coroner's inquests were as prevalent as ever and people continued to find ways of abruptly ending their lives.

This book is the second volume which looks at the subject of sudden deaths in Suffolk in the 19th century. It chronicles the period of time which encompassed the Crimean War and the start of the so-called Golden Age of Agriculture. The reports of the sudden deaths during this period are almost exclusively derived from the inquest reports in the county newspapers.

Geoffrey Robinson
November 2021

Note: The author make no apologies for the use of punctuation by the Victorian newspaper employees.

1851

Before we delve into our litany of sudden deaths occasioned by much misfortune, we might pause momentarily to remember that a woman in Victorian England faced many different challenges to modern-day women through her life from her infancy through marriage and childbirth to her old age. Here are three instances of the vicissitudes of a woman's life that should make us ponder.

Baby Found Dead in Bed
On May 28th 1851, at Worlingworth, an inquest was held on the body of the infant child of a single woman, Sarah Rose, which was found dead in bed. The child was nine weeks old. It appeared in evidence that the child had been sickly and ailing from its birth and subject to stoppages. From other testimony, it transpired that the woman had been a very kind and affectionate mother. The jury, feeling satisfied that the child died from natural causes, returned a verdict to that effect.

We can build up a picture of Sarah's circumstances from archival records. Sarah Rose lived with her father and two brothers in a small cottage by the former Worlingworth Green. The three men of the household were each described in the 1851 census as "ag lab and pauper" which suggests that they had little or no work. Sarah's younger brother Charles would die in the Melton Asylum in 1864. The inquest for the child's death would, in all likelihood, have taken place at the Swan Inn in Worlingworth. The great majority of those present – the jury members and the onlookers - would have known Sarah and her family. It must have been quite an ordeal for this 22 year old housekeeper.

Collapsed into Husband's Arms

Two days earlier, the Coroner, J.E. Sparrow Esq., had held an inquest at Gislingham on the body of 33 year old Dorothy Martin, the wife of Thomas Martin, a labourer. The poor woman had been confined for about a month and had hardly recovered. Standing before the fire, she suddenly fell into her husband's arms and died instantly. From the evidence of Mr. Downing, surgeon, who had been in attendance upon her, and was immediately called in, the bursting of a vessel on the lungs was the immediate cause of death. A verdict to that effect was returned.

Dead in Bed

The following day, at Somersham, an inquest was held on the body of Mary Green, widow, aged 84. The deceased lived alone in a room and was in the receipt of two shillings a week from the parish to maintain herself. The Union House had been offered her but she had refused. She was found dead in her bed, having about five minutes before been spoken to by a neighbour. Verdict: "Died by the visitation of God."

Death, Disease and the Visitation of God

For centuries, medical men struggled with the task of explaining the causes of death and disease. The basic functions of how a human body worked were a mystery. If a person died, based on the doctor's limited knowledge, the death might only have been described as a fever, apoplexy or convulsions, or what could be visibly seen such as a wound, or if there was evidence of an over-indulgent lifestyle.

Occasionally the cause of death would be described as "By the Visitation of God." During a more religious time, this meant that the death could not be explained and it was thought that God had decided that the person should die. This phrase "Visitation of God" later came to mean that the person had died of natural causes. It was a verdict that was often given at coroners inquests, especially in the 19th century. Post mortems were quite rare and doctors gave a medical opinion on the corpse, based on the visual evidence. The coroner was also interested in determining whether there was any criminality involved in the death. "By the Visitation of God" as an inquest verdict was a phrase that could be applied to many different circumstances of death.

In 1837, compulsory registration of births, marriages and deaths had been introduced. In order to bring some statistical order to the reports made by the Registrar-General on the numbers of such events, coroners were directed to make causes of death in more precise terms. "Visitation of God" was an unsatisfactory phrase which was to be replaced with more precise medical terms.

At first, the response nationwide was very slow so we find the term "Visitation of God" still in use in the early 1850s. In particular, where a coroner was not involved in investigating the death, many doctors still used the phrase. An example of the usage of this verdict continues our journey through the 1850s with an inquest held at Chelmondiston at the end of January 1851.

Visitation of God
On Thursday the 30th at Chelmondiston, on view of the body of Michael Catchpole aged 60. It was stated in evidence that the deceased, with his son Charles, and a man named Henry Hill, were dredging stone off the West Rocks on Monday last. About nine o'clock at night, they returned to Harwich harbour and dropped anchor just off the lights. On the following morning at half past five, the three men were engaged in raising the anchor, when the deceased exclaimed: "Charles, make haste, for I feel very sick and queerly," and dropped onto the deck. His son and Hill picked him up and found life extinct. They brought the boat to Pin Mill and carried the body home. Verdict, "Died by the Visitation of God."

Fatal diseases were never far away from the population as we hear from an inquest in March that year. We should bear in mind that the understanding of the causes of cholera was still at an early stage in the 1850s as this particular case demonstrates.

Cholera Outbreak
The inquest, held at Eriswell, was on the body of a boy named Gathercole, aged seven years, who had died of cholera. Mr. Harris, the surgeon, said he believed the exciting cause of the illness of the deceased to have been the deaths of some bullocks in a shed, not more than eight or ten yards from the cottage, and into which the family had to go to fetch turf.

The effluvia, arising from the animals dying in the shed, would certainly infect the air round it to a greater distance than the cottage. The shed was partly open, the opening standing diagonally with the cottage door. It ought to be whitewashed before anything else was put into it, and before the cottagers went there again. The jury returned a verdict accordingly.

In November of 1851, there were three inquests which demonstrated the fragility of life. Two of the inquests were held in the same parish. The first inquest proved once again the dangers inherent in carrying a loaded gun.

Accidentally Shot
On Saturday 22nd November, at Kettleburgh, on the body of Charles Hall, of that parish, labourer, aged 26 years. From the evidence of the witnesses, it was proved that Hall, who was not in work, had gone out with a gun in the morning of the Wednesday preceding, and about 12 o'clock beckoned to his younger brother who was at work in Mr. John Walker's barn, to come to him.

Upon going up, James discovered that Charles' clothes were on fire and Charles said he was shot in the left side of the body; that in going through a gate near the barn, the gate caught the gun, which was on the cock, and it went off and lodged the whole contents in his body. The poor man lingered until Friday night, when death put an end to his sufferings. Verdict, "Accidental death."

Hit by a Waggon
On the following Monday, at Framlingham, an inquest was held on the body of Benoni Mann, late an inmate of the Plomesgate Union-House at Wickham Market, aged 16 years. It appeared from the evidence of the witnesses examined, that in the afternoon

of Saturday the 15th, Mann was walking to Framlingham and overtook in Parham, one of Mr. Woods' coal waggons driven by William Fulcher.

Upon asking Fulcher for a ride, Fulcher at first refused, afterwards he consented, but did not stop his horses and Mann, in attempting to get on to the front of the waggon, slipped between the fore-bar and the off fore-wheel, which caused a lacerated wound from the knee for ten inches upwards and a most severe contusion. It was some little time before Fulcher could stop his horses and was then unable to extricate Mann without assistance. Mann was laid upon Fulcher's great coat in the coal waggon, covered with sacks and taken to Framlingham, where he was immediately attended by Mr. Wilson, surgeon, but in a few days, mortification came on and Mann died on November 23rd.

The Coroner reprimanded Fulcher for permitting this boy to get up while the waggon was in motion but he was known by the jury to be a very steady old man and long accustomed to the road. Verdict, "Accidental death."

The final inquest of November 1851 brought to light superstitions that still held sway in the daily lives of some country folk.

Country Witchcraft
On Tuesday at the same place (Framlingham), on the body of William Catchpole, aged two years and a half, the only child of John Catchpole, labourer, who lives rather more than a mile from the town. Several witnesses were examined in the course of a long

enquiry. From the evidence, it appeared that on Monday 10th, while Mrs. Catchpole was gone to an adjoining cottage with some bread to be baked (although not absent more than two minutes), the clothes of the child caught fire and he ran to the door which increased the flames, and in attempting to put out the fire himself, burnt both his hands very much. After the mother, with the assistance of a neighbour, had stripped the burning clothes from the poor child, a consultation was held by a houseful of old women as to what was to be done.

They decided that the child was to be carried into Framlingham, to a Mr. John Oakley there, who was to charm away the fire. This unfortunate child was accordingly taken to Mr. Oakley, who rubbed the child with his own spittle, muttering at the same time some cabbalistic words, which the witnesses could not understand and he told the mother "to do nothing with the child."

The following morning early on, Mr. Oakley went of his own accord to see the child again, because he thought he had not "done enough" and then repeated his charm. The child did not get better, notwithstanding the double charm, and in four days afterwards the mother took the child to Mr. Wilson, surgeon, who attended it instantly and continued to do so for several days. The tendons of the right hand being badly burnt, lockjaw came on about the 18th and death put an end to the child's sufferings on the 24th. Verdict, "Death from Accidental Burning."

Mr. Oakley was examined at great length but persisted in his power of being able to charm away fire from persons who have been burnt and he did not appear abashed by the ridicule of the Jury. It is a lamentable fact that in the middle of the nineteenth century, many of the poor people in that parish are still superstitious enough to believe in the power of this man's charms. It is not possible to say whether the life of this child could have been saved but, through the folly and superstition of his mother and her neighbours, four days had elapsed before any medical attendance was resorted to.

Old customs and superstitions still held sway in the rural Suffolk parish; change came slowly and not without resistance. Even in modern times, I recall the story of a local man who could charm away warts and this was in the 1950s and 60s. Parishioners today can still testify to the strange gift that had been bestowed upon him. It is unsurprising that those Framlingham women put their faith in the restorative powers of Mr. Oakley.

1852

In March 1852 the Ipswich Journal published the reports of two inquests relating to a drowning and a child burning to death. These modes of death probably constituted two of the most frequent types of accidental fatalities during the 19th century.

Drowned in a Ditch
We learn that, on Tuesday March 9th at Spexhall near Halesworth, 15 month old Harriet Page, the daughter of a labourer of that parish, was found drowned in a ditch of water at the bottom of the garden, a quarter of an hour after she had been seen playing in the wash-house. There was no evidence to show how the child got into the ditch, but the cause was believed to be accidental and the jury returned a verdict in accordance with those facts.

Clothes Ignited by the Fire
One week later, an inquest took place at Westleton, near Yoxford, into the sudden death of Elizabeth Barker, aged 6 years, the daughter of a labourer. It was proved that, on Friday 12th, the deceased was found lying dead at the step of the backhouse door of the cottage, with her clothes burnt off her body. It transpired that she had been left in charge of two younger children and that

whilst in the act of taking some vegetables off the fire, her clothes ignited. Verdict accordingly.

Baby Found in a Pond
Helmingham was in the spotlight in April 1852 when Coroner J.E. Sparrow, Esq., had to preside over two inquests. On the 24th April, an inquest was held into the discovery of a new-born female child found at the bottom of a pond, on the premises belonging to Mrs. Mary Kersey, of that parish. The body was discovered by Henry Cann, a labourer, tied up in a bundle of clothes, round which was wound a string, to which was attached a brick-bat. Circumstances gave rise to strong suspicion that a servant of Mrs. Kersey, named Amelia Tye, had given birth to the child.

From the state of decomposition in which the body was found, it was evident that it had been in the water many days. After evidence of these facts had been given, Mr. Blomfield, surgeon, clearly established that the child had never breathed and was stillborn. Upon this satisfactory testimony, the jury returned a verdict to the foregoing effect.

Schoolchild Burnt to Death
And on the 26th, in the same parish, on view of the body of Sarah Knights, aged 8 years, who died from injuries received from burning. This child was one of the pupils in the school established and supported by John Tollemache, Esq. The schoolmistress had just previously gone to dinner, leaving this child and others in the school room. The deceased, whilst endeavouring to dust the mantel-piece, came in contact with the grate and her clothes took fire. She rushed out into the park when she was met by the schoolmistress, who attempted to throw her upon the grass, and both fell.

Assistance was soon at hand and the fire was extinguished, but the child was so much injured about the chest, breast and neck that she survived only a few hours. Verdict, "Accidental death."

It might be of interest to the reader to learn that a pupil (or pupils) would be given sweeping, dusting and general cleaning duties in the schoolroom on a daily basis. For these menial tasks, each pupil would be given a few pence a week. This money, as part of the weekly income of a household, might have been vital in supporting the child's family.

We move on to September and a national event of great sorrow – the death of Arthur Wellesley, the Duke of Wellington, the victor over Napoleon at the Battle of Waterloo in 1815. In Suffolk, meanwhile, young and old were still finding ways of ending their own lives in bizarre ways and means.

Caught Fire in a Burning Field
At Needham Market, an inquest was held into the death of George Duffell Chester, aged 6 years, the son of a widow in that town. It appeared in evidence that, on the day before, the boy, instead of going to school, had wandered into a field where some weeds were burning. He sat down close to the fire and by some means or other his clothes caught fire.

His cries were heard by another boy in the same field who went to his assistance, together with a man named Robert Scarlett who was at work in an adjoining pasture. He put out the fire and carried the boy home. The poor sufferer was burned very much about the back and loins and lingered until the following day when he expired. Verdict, "Accidental death."

Suspicious Child Death in Witnesham

At Witnesham, there was a rare occurrence when a post-mortem examination was called for by the coroner. The inquest was concerned with the death of a four month old baby, Jemima Copping, the illegitimate daughter of Phoebe Copping of that parish, single woman. The child died very suddenly the preceding day without having any medical attendance and, this being the third illegitimate child of the same woman who had all died as infants, it was considered by the parish authorities highly necessary to have a public inquiry. By the direction of the coroner, Mr. Meadows of Otley, surgeon, made a post mortem examination of the body, taking out the stomach, which he afterwards opened in the presence of the jury. Every organ was found to be in a healthy state and the stomach contained nothing but milk. Mr. Meadows was therefore of the opinion that the infant died of congestion of the brain. The verdict recorded was "Natural death by the Visitation of God."

Those Witnesham men who served as jurors for that inquest probably did not expect to see an infant's corpse dissected in front of them. Yet many of them would have been farmers and used to the sight of the entrails of their livestock. Death, itself, was always close at hand in the rural community. There were no hospitals or nursing homes for the elderly poor. The workhouse was the only option outside of your parish. Infant childcare was primitive by today's standards. When there was a death in the parish, young or old, the funeral was a parish affair. There were no cremations; you joined the long list of inhabitants interred in the churchyard and the whole village generally came out to pay their respects or close their curtains as the funeral procession went past.

1853

At the beginning of January 1853, the Ipswich Journal was replete with a plethora of inquest reports that must have fascinated its readership with the sheer diversity of methods, deliberate or accidental, that those unfortunate people fell victim to.

Fatal Railway Accident

A fatal rail accident occurred on the evening of Christmas Day to Charles Jolly, a farm labourer in the employ of Mr. Johnson of Lakenheath Fen. An inquest was held by H. Wayman, Gent., when it transpired that the deceased had been drinking for over six hours at the Railway Tavern, close to the Mildenhall station, and at half past ten, he left "a little worse for liquor" for home, choosing the railway as the more direct route. After having proceeded a mile, he was struck by the mail train. The engine driver saw no one on the line, but felt a jerk. He did not stop but on reaching Ely station, he found some blood on the life-guard and some brains on a step. He must have been lying on the line when struck, for if he had been standing there would have been blood or some mark on the buffers or buffer plank, but there was none.

When found shortly afterwards, his body presented a frightfully mutilated aspect; his head was severed as if by a knife and his heart laid whole in another direction, his liver having clung to a carriage which deposited it at Ely. A verdict of "Accidental death" was returned, no blame whatever being imputed to the railway servants. The man was 24 years of age and unmarried. We sincerely trust that this will prove a warning to parties not to trespass upon the railway.

Suicide from Oxalic Acid
J.E. Sparrow, Esq., Coroner, was once again dashing around the eastern parishes of the county in January, as the two following reports indicate.

On Tuesday 11th at Somerleyton, near Lowestoft, on view of the body of Thomas Smith, aged 37. The deceased, who was a servant in the employ of S.M. Peto, Esq., M.P., was on the previous Saturday found dead in the engine-house, erected by the proprietor for the purpose of supplying the mansion with water. It appeared that the deceased had been in a state of intoxification for several days and it was supposed, from the circumstance of a mug which had contained oxalic acid being found near him, that he had taken a quantity of that deadly liquid. A post mortem examination made by Mr. Meadows of Lowestoft proved that this had been the fact. As it was believed that deceased was suffering from an attack of delirium tremens at the time, the jury brought in a verdict of "Temporary Insanity."

Struck by a Mill Sail
On the 12th at Rumburgh near Halesworth, on view of the body of Robert Searle, aged 69. It appeared from the evidence of Benjamin Sayer, son of Mr. Daniel Sayer, miller, of Rumburgh, that the

deceased had come to the mill for corn, and was in the act of taking some hay delivered to him by the witness from a cart standing under the mill. The mill was at full work under gale, and the unfortunate deceased, notwithstanding a caution to be careful from the witness, was struck on the left breast by one of the sails and thrown to a distance of 32 yards. When picked up, life was extinct. Verdict, "Accidental death."

Suicide by Chemical Ingestion

At Buxhall near Stowmarket, there was an unusual case of sudden death by poisoning. The inquest took place in the parish on the 14th January, before C. Gross, Gent., Coroner, on the body of Jane Dykes, aged 19, the wife of John Dykes, labourer, who had died from the effects of taking corrosive sublimate, also known as mercuric chloride. From the evidence it appeared that Dykes was married to his wife last Whitsuntide and that since that time they had lived together on good terms, notwithstanding his being under the necessity of seeking medical advice, caused by his immoral conduct. He obtained from a quack in a neighbouring parish a quantity of the poison, which he kept in a box in his bedroom.

On Tuesday 5th the deceased went into the room and on her return told her husband that she had taken some of the stuff out of the bottle in his chest. Upon hearing this, he immediately sent his mother (who lives under the same roof) to the deceased, and started off himself to Stowmarket for medical assistance. On the arrival of the surgeon, an emetic was administered and the deceased at first appeared to get better, but ultimately the symptoms returned and on the 13th she died. During her sufferings she repeatedly told those that visited her there was no blame attached to her husband. A post mortem examination had been made by Mr. Harling, who stated that the deceased died solely from the effects of the poison. The jury came to the verdict that the deceased came to her death by poison administered by her own hands, but what was the state of her mind at that time there was no evidence to show. Corrosive sublimate was used to treat syphilis before the advent of antibiotics.

The following month, February, brought to the attention of the newspaper reader three of the commonest means of sudden death in Suffolk – a child burnt to death, a drowning and a fatal accident involving a threshing machine. Nevertheless one suspects that the reports would have equally horrified and fascinated the reader.

Children Burnt in Cottage
At Sutton on February 3rd, an inquest was held into the death of Caroline Woodward, aged five years, daughter of Daniel Woodward, of that parish, labourer. It was as far back as January 5th that Mrs. Woodward, the mother, went to the village shop for some trifling articles, leaving her three children alone in the house. Soon afterwards, a neighbour heard some screams and ran to the cottage to find the girl Caroline enveloped in flames, which she extinguished as quickly as possible. Mr. Walker of Alderton was immediately sent for and was in instant attendance upon the child until February 2nd, when she died. Verdict, "Death from accidental burning."

Man Drowned in Pond
On Friday morning the 4th February, at about seven o'clock, as Daniel Chaplin, thatcher, of Great Finborough, was about to get a pail of water from a pond in his garden, he observed a man's hat lying near the edge of the water, and also a basket and stick standing in his garden within three or four yards of the pond.

Chaplin immediately called his neighbours, when, on raking the pond, they found the dead body of a labourer belonging to the adjoining parish of Buxhall, named James Ranson.

An inquest was held in the afternoon before Charles Gross, Gent., Coroner, when it appeared that the deceased had on the previous day been to Stowmarket and purchased a basket of shop goods, and that on his return he called in at the Shepherd and Dog at Onehouse where he remained some time; that he afterwards called in at the White Horse at Great Finborough, where he had a pint of gin and beer, and he remained there till about twelve o'clock, when he started for home quite intoxicated.

It is supposed that the deceased lost his way, the night being very dark, and wandered into Chaplin's garden, where he fell over some low paling into the pond. It was stated that the deceased was in the habit of getting drunk, of wandering about in a strange way and there was no doubt that he had accidentally fallen into the pond. The jury found a verdict accordingly. The deceased was a married man, about 70 years of age, and he left an aged wife.

Frock Caught in Rotating Spindle
On the 9th February, at the Suffolk General Hospital, an inquest was held on the body of David Scates, labourer, aged 23 years, in the employ of Samuel Payne of Hawstead. On the previous Monday, he was engaged in removing straw from a threshing machine when the spindle caught his frock and wound him round, and before the horses could be stopped, dashed his head against the floor of the barn. He was released as quickly as possible and removed in an insensible state to the hospital, where he was attended by C.C. Smith, Esq., surgeon. He never rallied but died in about three hours. It appeared that, about four years since, a young

man was badly injured by being caught by the same spindle; and the jury, in returning a verdict of "Accidental death" expressed a hope that Mr. Payne will endeavour to erect some covering over the spindle, to prevent such accidents in future.

This last inquest report contains many interesting points: for example, working practices using horses to drive machinery, the clothing still worn by labourers and the application or otherwise of suitable safety measures. It also paints a picture of the frailties of economic life on the farm.

Woman Burnt to Death
One month later, in March, another death through burning occurred but this time it was the mother, Susan Thurman, who was consumed by fire, not the children. The evidence heard at the inquest related how two families, the Thurmans and the Ramsys occupied two cottages under one roof upon the hill near the Kyson Dock at Woodbridge.

On Wednesday, Ramsy and his wife were both at work in the fields; William Thurman was also at his work, leaving Mrs. Thurman with only some children in the house. About three o'clock in the afternoon, they ran screaming into the fields, and gave an alarm that Mrs. Thurman was burnt to death.

William Thurman, an intelligent little boy, said that his mother was putting the boiler on to the fire and her clothes suddenly caught fire and blazed up; that they both tried to put the fire out and he was much burnt in doing so. His mother soon fell down into a basket of linen, which also caught fire. Upon the daughter and other persons going in, the 43 year old mother of four was found to be dead and the linen still burning. The body presented a dreadful object to the jury. Verdict, "Accidentally burnt to death."

Drowned in the Deben
July 1853 may have been a rather wet month in Suffolk as we read about an abnormal river level at Debenham which claimed the life of a young boy. The inquest in that village concerned the sudden death by drowning of nine year old Thomas Garrod, the son of William Garrod, labourer.

On the afternoon of the 14th, this little boy was upon a footbridge across the river Deben, looking at the water, which had risen more than six feet. In playing with a stick in the water, his foot slipped and he fell off the bridge in sight of his mother and others and was immediately swept away by the flood; his body was not found until the following morning. Verdict, "Accidentally drowned."

In November 1853, we learn once again of the everyday pitfalls of drinking and driving a cart. The newspaper report, of the sort repeated many times throughout that period, served to highlight a serious social problem.

Drunk and Driving a Cart
On Tuesday last, at Brandeston, on the body of William Boon, of that parish, aged 49. It appeared that Boon, who was a common carter, took a load of corn to Woodbridge on Monday and was returning in the evening with half a ton of coals. He had been drinking there and stopped at Charsfield Horseshoes, where he had some gin and beer with two neighbours.

About seven o'clock he was found lying in the road near Hoo Schoolhouse, almost insensible, by a boy returning from his work.

The boy fetched a lantern and other persons came up, among them Robert Smith of Earl Soham, who, knowing Boon, took him into his cart. Boon was then unable to speak. He was alive when going through Kettleburgh but died before reaching his own house. He had received so severe a blow upon his right temple as to force off some of his hair. The horse and cart were afterwards found near the Kettleburgh watermill and the Jury, having no doubt that he fell off the cart and pitched on his head, returned a verdict of "Accidental Death."

1854

Whilst studying the reports of sudden deaths in 1854, a short paragraph in a January edition of the Ipswich Journal caught the eye. Although the report of the death carried little of the sensationalism often experienced, it tells its own story about life at the very lowest level of Victorian society and was worthy of inclusion in this text.

Inmate at Oulton Workhouse

One Sunday in January, an idiot pauper named Henry Mingay died at Oulton Workhouse. He belonged to the parish of Lowestoft and was admitted with his mother on the 13th December 1785, into the above establishment where he continued as an inmate until his decease. At a moderate calculation, he has, during his 68 years residence, cost the parish £450.

Loaded Gun Discharged

Returning to our theme of sudden deaths and the early months of 1854, we learn of a terrible accident involving another loaded gun which resulted in the loss of a husband and father. On the morning of the 4th January, Mr. John Thurston, a nurseryman at Brockford, 44 years of age, was removing a loaded gun from an oven where it had been placed to dry. By some means, it went off and the contents were lodged in his breast. He had only time to exclaim, "I am shot, I am shot – I am dead," when he expired, leaving a widow and three small children to lament the loss of a good husband and tender father.

The deceased was a most industrious and scientific gardener, having through his exertions obtained several prizes at flower and other shows, and was most highly respected by the gentry, clergy, and others for his industry and perseverance in business. His loss will be much felt not only by his family but by many around him.

In the same month, we learn of a serious case of alcoholism. Addiction to drink was a common theme when sudden deaths were reported in the newspapers, even though the death from alcoholism was not altogether unexpected. The details were quite shocking, even for the time.

Alcohol-induced Death

On Thursday 5th January, at the Cricketer's Arms, in the parish of St. Margaret, an inquest was held on the body of Elizabeth Cole, aged 44. The deceased was of intemperate habits and had been under the influence of drink for five successive weeks. On the Wednesday, a little after 3 o'clock, she was left by her husband, who is a shoemaker, in bed, having been drunk ever since Christmas Day. She was in a state of stupor, a condition into which she usually passed after long drinking.

At five o'clock, when her husband returned home, he found her dead, lying in the same position as when he left. It further appeared that the wretched creature had been addicted to drink for fourteen years, and that, though visited by such an affliction, the husband had been generally kind and considerate. The jury returned a verdict of "Found dead, there being not sufficient evidence as to the cause of death."

Cut Throat with Razor
January 1854 also saw a horrendous occurrence take place at Chelmondiston. On Friday 20th January an inquest was held at the Butt and Oyster public-house, on view of the body of Rachael, the wife of Mr. Lucas Charles King, mariner, of that parish, aged 39. The circumstances of the case were very painful. The deceased gave birth to a son on the 3rd and from that time until the 19th had been slowly recovering, but was in a very dejected state of mind.

On the Wednesday night she passed in a very restless state; on Thursday morning, about nine o'clock, she requested her nurse to call her little boy, a child about 12 years of age. She whispered to him and he went downstairs and returned and gave his mother something into her hand, which the nurses could not see. Soon afterwards, they heard a "ruttling" in her throat. Being alarmed, they turned down the bedclothes and found that the poor woman had inflicted an extensive wound in her throat with a razor. She died in about two minutes.

It came out in evidence that the deceased had desired her child to fetch a razor that she might cut her corns, and that in completing the dreadful act, she completely eluded the attention of the nurses. After a short deliberation, the jury returned a verdict of "Temporary insanity."

We now turn to the distressing subject of child deaths through burning and ask the question "Was there a preponderance of child deaths through burning in the winter months?" It might have been the case but without the statistics, if any were kept on such a gruesome subject, we cannot be certain. What is certain is that two young children came by their deaths in such circumstances within days of each other in February 1854.

Child Burnt to Death

On the 24th February, an inquest was held at Parham, on the body of Abel Barham, aged eight years, the second son of Francis Barham, of that parish, who was so badly burnt on Wednesday afternoon during the temporary absence of his mother, that he died the following morning. Mrs. Barham had been in the habit of leaving her children, and when remonstrated with for doing so, said they were left in charge of her daughter; but she being only a year older, was totally incompetent to render any assistance to her brother when his clothes caught fire in attempting to take off the boiler. Verdict, "Accidentally burnt."

Another Child Burnt to Death

Then at Sternfield a week later, on the body of William Boast, aged four years, son of William Boast, of that parish, labourer. From the evidence of Mr. Gilbert, a neighbour, it appeared that Mrs. Boast went out on the morning of the Thursday preceding, leaving this and three other children in her cottage, with a fire. She had scarcely left the house, when this child was seen standing at the door all in flames. Mrs. Gilbert threw down the child and smothered the flames with a rug. Mr. Freeman, surgeon, attended the child but he was so much burnt that he died early the following morning. Verdict, "Accidentally burnt."

Threshing Machine Death

A threshing machine claimed the life of another labourer at Hundon in March. The inquest, held on the 14th March, described how Thomas Brown, of Cowlinge, a father of seven children, was working on a steam threshing machine while at work on the farm of Mr. Keeble, at Hundon Great Lodge. In attempting to step over the machinery, his foot slipped and the lower part of his leg was completely cut off. The poor man was removed to the Lodge where amputation of the remaining part of the leg was as soon as possible resorted to but he died before the surgeons (Mr. Stutter of Wickhambrook, Mr. Barnes and Mr. Martin of Clare) could close the wound. Verdict, "Accidental Death."

Gossip on Ill-Treatment

During the same month, an inquest was held at Wickham Market from which a verdict of "Death by the Visitation of God" was reached. However, this case was more complicated and perhaps even controversial in the town, than the verdict portrays.

The inquest took place on a Tuesday evening; the deceased was an 18 month old infant, Emily Dale, youngest daughter of George Dale, stonemason. This child died early on the preceding Saturday morning and would have been buried in due time but for some idle gossips having circulated a report that the child had, on Friday afternoon, been ill treated by Ellen Scase, the nurse girl. The parish officers therefore sent for the coroner. Several witnesses were examined at the inquest but nothing was alleged against the girl Scase, except that when the child cried on Friday afternoon, she took it up and shook it and nipped its nose. Another witness said that she slapped the child's face. Mr. Muriel, however, who attended the child just previous to her death, said that the child died from excessive diarrhoea and a weakly constitution.

In presenting this particular case in this book, it was felt that it might add to the story if it could be determined what happened to Ellen Scase. A concerted attempt was made to trace what happened to her in later life. Even allowing for the misspelling of her surname, efforts have returned a blank – no marriage, no entry in the 1861 census and no apparent death. In 1861 her parents were living by themselves on the Hill in Wickham Market.

Ellen's reputation must have suffered from the result of the inquest proceedings even though the allegations of cruelty to the child were largely ignored by the inquest. One should remember that a number of local people would have attended the inquest as onlookers. Then there was the jury of between twelve and eighteen local men. Ellen might have found herself out of work soon after the inquest. If she could not get another position and if she had no other source of income, she might have ended up in the Plomesgate Union Workhouse and a very uncertain future.

The summer months of 1854 turned up some sudden deaths which proved once again that old adage "in the midst of life, we are in death." Bell-ringing and gleaning were once essential aspects of rural village life and yet ordinary folk could still be struck down in the most ordinary of circumstances.

Collapsed after Bell-Ringing
In June at Hintlesham, John Woods and four other men were ringing the bells in the church one Monday morning. After finishing the peal, which occupied about twenty minutes, Woods sat down on a stool to rest and immediately afterwards fell dead

into the arms of a fellow ringer. Mr. Growse, surgeon, of Hadleigh, who was summoned to attend the deceased, was of the opinion that apoplexy was the cause of death and the Jury returned a verdict accordingly. The deceased was only 46 years of age.

Child Death after Gleaning
In late September, soon after the harvest had been taken in, an inquest was held at Framlingham on the body of Eliza Fairweather, aged 12 years, daughter of John Fairweather, labourer. This little girl had been gleaning the day before and in the afternoon was taken ill in a field, some distance from the town. She was put into a cart to be carried home but died on the road.

There was a report that she had been struck by her little brother on the previous Monday, but the evidence given before the jury proved that, up to the time of her being taken ill, she was in her usual good health and ate a hearty supper on the Wednesday night. The verdict given was "Natural death by the visitation of God."

Expired at Grandson's Funeral
Then, in October, at Grundisburgh, an inquest was held on the body of 67 year old Harriet Long, who on the previous day had been following the body of her grandson to the grave and, before the procession had reached the churchyard, she suddenly dropped down and expired in a matter of minutes. Verdict, "Sudden death by the Visitation of God."

If there was ever an instance of sudden death which would have frightened and perplexed the family, friends and neighbours of a deceased person, then the example of Harriet Long's expiration must have raised many questions for the rector of Grundisburgh to answer.

We bring the year 1854 to a dispiriting end with the abject story of a young boy who lost his life in the days leading up to Christmas. The coroner had to leave his home on Christmas Day to travel to Benhall to oversee the resulting inquest. No matter what the day of the year was, every inquest was a matter of life and death for the relatives of a deceased person.

Impaled by a Pitchfork
The inquest took place in front of Mr. John Wood, Esq., Coroner, on Monday 25th December, at Benhall, on the body of Robert Goddard, aged 14 years, a boy in the employ of Mr. William Robinson, farmer. Goddard was loading straw on a cart on the Wednesday preceding, and when the horse moved forward, the whole load slipped off, taking the boy with it and the pitchfork, which he had in his hand, ran into his body. Medical aid was immediately procured but after suffering for thirty-three hours, he died on Friday morning. Verdict, "Accidental death."

1855

Bringing together a large number of newspaper inquest reports in one book throws light on many different aspects of life in Victorian Suffolk. The year 1855 turned out to be no exception. We begin the year with a January visit to Eye and the Union Workhouse.

Eye Workhouse Death
The inquest was held at the Workhouse on the body of Fidele Macon, a Frenchwoman aged 60. On Tuesday the 9th January she was admitted into the house in a state of destitution. She complained of hunger and the Governor gave her 6 ozs. of bread and 1 oz. of cheese, which allowance was repeated at six thirty in the evening. Both allowances were eaten with great greediness and at half past eleven on the Wednesday night she died, after a succession of fits, caused by indigestion, as it was afterwards shown by the evidence of Mr. Miller and Mr. Ashford. The Jury returned a verdict of "Death by the Visitation of God."

It should be noted how strict the Governor was in giving an exact allowance of food to the unexpected visitor. It would be futile to speculate why a Frenchwoman was wandering around Suffolk.

Buried in a Pit

A simple case of another accident in the workplace led to a sudden death in Wrentham. On Wednesday 11th January, James Peck, a labourer aged 65, was digging in a pit when the earth caved in and he was buried. He was dug out the same day and carried home where he died of the injuries he had received. The jury at the inquest returned a verdict of "Accidental death."

Drowned in a Well

A few days earlier at the White Hart Inn, Southgate Street in Bury St Edmunds, an inquest was held on the body of Mary Wells, 80, who was found drowned in a well. It appeared from the evidence that a neighbour Susannah Grey went to draw water on the morning of the 3rd, and saw a hand at the bottom of the well. She gave the alarm and a person of the name of Mingay who was passing at the time, went down into the well and found deceased quite dead, lying on her right side. It is presumed that deceased, who was subject to fits of giddiness, must have had an attack just as she was reaching over the well to pull back the lid, and thus fell in and was drowned. Verdict, "Accidental Death."

Impoverished Death

On March 26th, at Gazeley, an inquest was held before G.A. Partridge, Esq. Coroner for the Liberty of Bury St Edmunds, on the body of William Nunn, labourer, who died on the previous Saturday. From the evidence of his widow and a neighbour, it appeared that the deceased was 28 years of age and had been ailing for a long time.

Since harvest, he had been receiving a stone of flour weekly from the Guardians, and five shillings from the Newmarket Provident Club, until seven weeks ago, when Mr. Faircloth, the medical officer of the club, visited him and the club money was stopped. His wife then applied to the Board of Guardians and obtained an extra half stone of flour and half a crown for one week but it was afterwards stopped. They were offered the Workhouse but refused to go in, the man declaring that he would sooner starve.

Mr. Kerry, surgeon of the parish, stated that he had attended the deceased as a member of his medical club and had returned him to the Board weekly as "unable to work" till the last fortnight when the deceased told him that his club pay had been stopped and he would try to work.

Mr. Kerry made a post mortem examination and found disease of the heart and congestion of the liver and lungs, but the body was well nourished and the muscle of good colour, which emphatically contradicted the statements that he had died from starvation. The Rev. T. Burroughes, Guardian of Gazeley parish, deposed that the outdoor allowance was stopped on the opinion of Mr. Faircloth, that the deceased was able to work. Verdict, "Natural death."

Drank from the Spout of a Kettle
In April on Monday 2nd, the Coroner for the Borough of Ipswich, Simon B. Jackaman, Esq., was called to the Portobello Inn in the parish of St. Margaret for an inquest held into the death of Ann Sadd aged two years. The father of the child, Robert Sadd, was a hawker and, with his wife and children, occupied a cottage in the parish and were said to be people of good conduct.

In the absence of the parents on the previous Saturday, the deceased drank from the spout of a kettle which was standing by the fire, her sister Anne, aged seven years, having taken hold of the handle and inclined the kettle forward. It further appeared that the kettle was always kept boiling by the children. When the father and mother returned home, they were greatly shocked, especially the latter, who was within a few days of her confinement. Every assistance was rendered by Mr. Adams, surgeon, to the unfortunate child but without avail, as she died on Sunday morning. The jury returned a verdict: "Death from being accidentally scalded by drinking boiling water from a tea kettle."

Fell Out of Boat and Drowned
Two drownings took up some of the column inches in August editions of the Ipswich Journal. Simon Batley Jackaman, Coroner, was once more called upon to hold an inquest into the death of George Young, a fifteen year old youth. This Saturday inquest was held at the Union Jack, St. Mary Key and described how, on the Friday evening at about half past eight, the deceased and a man named Fenn got into a boat moored off the Custom House. They proceeded across the dock with her to the Flint Wharf.

The deceased stood on the thwarts and, as he was sculling the boat along, the oar slipped and the deceased fell into the water. Fenn called out loudly for help and a man came up in a boat from the Flint Wharf. It did not appear that the deceased could swim and Fenn, who was never on the water before, was too frightened to attempt a rescue. The body was not recovered until eleven o'clock the same night. The Jury returned a verdict of "Accidentally drowned."

Drowned Attempting to Swim
The second drowning occurred near Woodbridge on Friday 17th August. During that afternoon, William Lambert, shoemaker, of Woodbridge, aged 23 years, went with two companions to bathe in the river at a place called "Hackney" in Melton. Whilst

attempting to learn to swim, he was carried by the ebb tide out of his depth and unfortunately drowned. George Worledge, in attempting to save him, narrowly escaped sharing the same fate. At the inquest held before Mr. Wood the following morning, a verdict of "Accidentally drowned" was returned. Lambert had been married for a year and left a widow with one child.

There were a spate of sudden deaths in December 1855. A millwright choked on a piece of beef-steak at the Chequers Inn, Boxford; an old woman and a six year old were separately burnt to death in incidents involving the hearth and a 72 year old labourer of Grundisburgh threw himself into a pond and drowned. But perhaps the death which was given the most column inches in the newspapers once again involved alcohol and illustrated the perils of the demon drink.

Addicted to Drink and Drove a Cart
The inquest was held at the Farnham George & Dragon on the body of Jeremiah Brunning, aged 66 years, who was found dead upon the turnpike road in the adjoining parish of Stratford St. Andrew in the afternoon two days previously. Brunning was a residential servant of Mr. Henry Cupper of Benhall, where he had lived for forty years. That morning he had been to Woodbridge with corn and was returning home with three tons of coals. He was unfortunately addicted to drinking and was found to have stopped at Marlesford Bell and Glemham Lion on his way home.

At about five o'clock, a waggon with four horses was observed by Mr. James Birt of Farnham, to be passing through the main street of that parish without any driver. After Mr. Birt had ascertained that the waggon belonged to Mr. Cupper, he went back on the road as quickly as possible and discovered a man lying dead in the road, with his head smashed in as if by the wheels of a waggon. The body was immediately taken to the Farnham George and identified as that of Mr. Brunning. Upon examining the road early on the following morning, it appeared as if the body had been dragged for twenty yards along the road before the wheels went over his head, both the ears having been cut off and the body presenting a shocking spectacle.

Mr. Cupper gave Brunning a most excellent character but admitted he was addicted to drinking. The night was excessively cold and there was some difference of opinion among the jury whether he fell off the waggon from the severity of the weather or the effects of drink. The verdict arrived at was "Accidental death."

1856

Britain came to the end of a bloody war on the Crimean peninsula during 1856. The Treaty of Paris was signed at the end of March thus bringing the Crimean War to an end. Two months earlier, Queen Victoria had instituted the Victoria Cross, awarded to honour those who had performed acts of valour during the war. As with the end of all major conflicts that Britain was involved in, the nation duly celebrated. At the time that the Queen was instituting that famous medal, another far more melancholy act was taking place in the parkland of Euston Hall, the seat of His Grace the Duke of Grafton.

Fell Through the Ice Whilst Skating

Mr. Ramsey Paramore, a young gentleman, aged 18, who had been spending Christmas with his uncle, the Rev. Arthur Dunlap at Bardwell, left the rectory to enjoy a day's skating in the park, about four miles distant. He was accompanied by Mr. Charles Cooper of Euston. They had skated around the shallow part for a short time when Mr. Paramore, carried away by too much eagerness, struck out into the centre of the lake when in an instant the ice gave way, and he was immersed in deep water. He rose twice and made vain efforts to save himself, the ice being too weak immediately around him. Mr. Cooper, after trying ineffectually to reach him, skated to the shore and ran for help to a group of labourers at work close by. They dragged a boat to the spot, breaking the ice as they went on, but the unfortunate youth had already disappeared and by the time the body was recovered nearly ten minutes had elapsed, when life was quite extinct.

The inquest returned a verdict of "Accidental death." The body of the unfortunate young man was consigned to the grave in Bardwell churchyard and the principal neighbours, to whom he had much endeared himself, accompanied his remains to their last resting place. This mournful event which had thus called away so suddenly in the prime of his age, a youth of much promise and amiable disposition, added another to the many sad proofs of the uncertainty of life and threw a general gloom over the whole neighbourhood.

Impaled on a Fork
A nasty accident occurred in Mendlesham during April 1856, to a lad named Albert Burch. He was in the employment of Mr. Spencer Gissing, farmer, and with a companion went with a horse and tumbril to procure a load of straw, to be put down in a bullock yard. Burch, whilst on the load as it was being conveyed to the yard, stuck his fork in the straw and lay down. Another lad, named James Fellingham, also employed by Mr. Gissing, saw the tumbril coming and opened the gate leading into the yard. He then went to the tumbril and pulled out what is called the "toe stick." The consequence was that the body of the vehicle kicked up and Burch was thrown out. We regret to say that one of the prongs of his fork entered the back of his head and penetrated his brain. He died on the following morning.

An inquest was held on the following Monday; Fellingham appeared exceedingly sorry for what he had done, saying he only did it for a "lark." It is a trick often played on farms. The Coroner, C. Gross Esq., reprimanded him but as the act was not done with malicious intent, Fellingham was ordered to be discharged.

Died in a Hedge

A singular death occurred near Troston in May. The inquest, held at Troston on the body of Jacob Goddard, an old man of 80 years of age, heard the following details. It appeared that the old man had been living in the Union House at Bury St Edmunds but he had walked to Troston Heath on Whit Monday to visit his son. On Tuesday morning he left his son's house to return to Bury but at about nine o'clock he was seen by a labourer named James Farrance, to leave the road and turn into a meadow in the direction of the place where his body was found, quite dead, on Friday afternoon.

He appears to have tried to get over or through a whitethorn hedge where there was no gap and, falling on a bough, was unable to recover himself, and remained there with his head hanging down on one side and his feet on the other, till his dead body was found. Mr. Green, surgeon, of Ixworth, examined the body and found every appearance of death having resulted from congestion of the brain, produced by being suspended with the head downwards. Verdict: "Accidental Death."

Collapsed Whilst Step-Dancing?

Newspaper reports of the many inquests held around the county sometimes would throw up a minor detail which might be evidence of an old Suffolk tradition. Thus the report of an inquest at the Maybush Inn, Waldringfield hinted at the possibility of "step dancing" being performed. The report went thus:

Mary Bloomfield, the wife of John Bloomfield, of Hemley, labourer, went on Wednesday afternoon to the Maybush Inn to see after her daughters, where she joined the dancers. After two or three rounds, she sat down; in two or three minutes she got up again, walked across the room and fell down dead without uttering a word. Verdict, "Natural death by the Visitation of God."

Threshing Machine Drum Broke
The inevitable threshing machine accident occurred in Wherstead in late May. For once, the subsequent death was the result of mechanical failure rather than a human error. The inquest was held at the Greyhound Inn, St. Matthew, on Saturday, upon the body of a man named William Cattermole, who met with his death under the following circumstances.

On the 28th May, deceased, who was in the employ of Mr. Leonard Wrinch of Erwarton, went to attend to the working of a steam threshing machine, belonging to his master, at Bourne Hall, Wherstead. Deceased was engaged in feeding, when suddenly the drum of the machine broke, one of the pieces striking him in the forehead, knocking him down backwards. Upon his fellow workmen picking him up, he found the frontal bone broken, and forced inwards towards the brain.

Mr. Bartlett, surgeon, was sent for, and directed the poor fellow's removal to the East Suffolk Hospital, where he died on Saturday morning from the effects of the injuries he had received. Verdict: "Accidental death."

Bitten by a Horse

In June, a most extraordinary attack was carried out by a horse, resulting in the sudden death of a labourer. On Wednesday morning, June 18th, as a labouring man named John Grice, in the employ of Mr. Phillips, of Ilketshall St Andrew, farmer, was unharnessing a horse from a plough, the animal suddenly turned upon him and seized him in such a manner that the back of his head and neck were grasped within its jaws.

Some men who were ploughing in the same field ran to the poor fellow's assistance, but on their approaching, the horse threw him down and knelt heavily on him; one of the men then struck the animal with a whipple-tree, when it got up and ran across the field where it was afterwards secured without difficulty. On attempting to raise Grice from the ground, he was found to be dead.

Crushed to Death on the Railway

The railway network was never out of the news with branch lines being steadily built all over the county. Accidents were also frequent as in this report of a fatality at Ipswich in July.

Yesterday morning Stephen Murrell, a porter at the goods shed of the Eastern Counties Railway station in this town, met with a frightful accident, resulting in instantaneous death. It appeared that he was engaged with four other men, in unloading a truck of stone. They had raised it from the truck, and were about to back a drag underneath to lower the stone upon, when the crane capsized from being over-weighted.

Murrell, instead of being in his proper place on the platform of the crane, had got in between the framing, and the consequence was that on the weight-box shifting, he was crushed to death. An inquest was held on his body at the Eastern Union Railway Hotel yesterday afternoon, before S.B. Jackaman, Esq., Coroner, when the above facts were given in evidence. Mr. Webster Adams, surgeon, who was sent for by Mr. Dorling, the district superintendent, immediately after the occurrence of the accident, described the nature of the poor fellow's injuries, showing that he was mutilated in the most frightful manner. In witness's opinion, the immediate cause of death was the injury to the viscera of the chest and abdomen.

At the conclusion of the evidence, the Coroner remarked that it appeared the machine broke from being over-weighted, but it was quite clear that the death of the deceased arose from an imprudent act on his own part – his being in a position in which he ought not to have been. Verdict: "Accidental death."

As usual during the summer months, there were a number of incidents of near drownings and fatalities in the county's waterways. A particularly sad incident of drowning took place on the River Orwell at the end of July.

Drowned in the Orwell
On August 1st an inquest was held at the Ship Launch, Ipswich, on the body of Charles Barwell, aged 21 years, in the employ of Messrs. Ransome and Sims, who met with his death in the following circumstances: George Dynes, a lad, deposed – I knew the deceased. I was bathing in the River Orwell, near Greenwich Farm, today, between 1 and 2 o'clock, and saw the deceased also bathing. I heard him call out "Robert, Robert." I swam towards

him as quickly as I could. On reaching the place where I last saw him, he had sunk, and I endeavoured to feel him with my feet. Whilst doing so, I saw a boat going down the river, with two men on it. It passed close by and I called out to the men "Come here – there's a man drowning." "Get him out yourself, you silly ---," (using a repulsive epithet) was the reply. I don't know who they were. When I first saw the deceased, he was swimming easily but he suddenly seemed unable to swim. I believe he was drowned accidentally. I tried all I could to save him but, having only one arm, I am not able to swim fast.

Joseph Symonds, who was at the bathing-place at the time and swam across the river with Mr. King of Rose Hill, to the assistance of the deceased, stated that Mr. King succeeded in finding the body lying at the bottom. There was not more than 3 or 4 feet of water at the spot at the time; at high water there would be about 8 feet. The place where the body was found was quite clear and sandy – no weeds. A verdict of "Accidentally Drowned whilst Bathing" was then returned. The Jury expressed an opinion that measures should be taken to prevent persons bathing at the spot where the deceased was drowned, many accidents having already occurred there. The above accident is rendered the more lamentable by the fact that deceased had only recently been married.

Suffocated Down a Well

In August, an accident occurred at the Waterloo Mill, Bramfield, to a miller named Edward Barber, employed by Mr. Higham of Wenhaston, the circumstances connected with which were singularly distressing. We are informed that a well was being sunk near the mill and that the men engaged in sinking it had already progressed so far in the undertaking as to have deepened it 65 feet. Upon the day mentioned, the interior of the well was found to be saturated, more or less, with mephitic or noxious gases, so much so that the men were afraid to descend to their work. Barber being on the spot at the time, and having descended on several previous occasions, volunteered to go down, and he was accordingly lowered, standing in a perpendicular position, having his foot in a noose and grasping the rope with his hand above.

He appeared to have reached the bottom without any signs of the approach of death; but while there those standing above thought they heard a faint groan, and they immediately began to draw him towards the mouth of the well; but after having drawn him about five or six feet from the bottom, he suddenly fell, and there being nothing at hand to assist the unhappy man out, he remained at the bottom of the well about an hour. He was then drawn up and life was found to be quite extinct. He is spoken of as a man of industrious and honest habits, and has left a young wife and a family of three children to deplore his untimely end.

The sinking and maintenance of water wells was just another occupational hazard in an increasingly industrialised age. A second accident involving a well occurred in Bury St. Edmunds during August.

Hit by a Bucket of Gravel in a Well
On the 29th August, at the Suffolk General Hospital, an inquest was convened upon the body of William Reynolds, labourer. From the evidence of William Tuck, a fellow labourer, it appeared that he, with deceased, his brother, and a little boy, were cleaning out a well at the back of the Cornwallis Inn, Brackland, Bury St. Edmunds on

Wednesday the 27th; and the usual bucket proving too large, they procured two pails for the purpose of bringing up the gravel and bricks which were at the bottom of the well. One pail came safe to its destination, but on drawing up the second bucket, it gave way and fell with its contents from a height of forty feet, onto the head of the unfortunate deceased. Tuck then let the brother down who found deceased groaning; and, after some little time, the sufferer was brought to the surface, when he was found to be covered in blood, and his hair falling off from very severe cuts on the head. He was afterwards conveyed to the Hospital and although Mr. Kilner, one of the surgeons, immediately attended him, the poor man expired on the Thursday morning from the effect of his wounds. Verdict "Accidental Death."

Crushed by Waggon Wheels
Another sudden death in the month of August came down to the frequent and misguided practice of riding on the shafts of a waggon. The inquest took place at Stratford St. Andrew on the body of James Hamby aged 17 years. Hamby was in the service of Mr. Robert Symonds, farmer, and was on the previous Friday, at about two o'clock, going with an empty waggon, drawn by a spirited mare, to fetch a load of oats.

John Pratt, who was at that time lying under a shock of corn, heard the waggon coming very rapidly down the road and saw the mare attempt (with the waggon behind her) to leap the gate, which was of course shattered to atoms. Hamby was at that time standing on the shafts, but was either thrown off or jumped down directly after passing the gate, and either fell immediately or was knocked down by the near wheels which passed over his head and killed him on the spot. Verdict, "Accidental death."

Fell Out of Window
Just occasionally, the report of a sudden death in the columns of the newspaper caught one's eye because of the bizarre nature of the death. At Halesworth, an inquest was held at the Swan Inn, touching on the death of an old lady named Esther Sones, who lived on Pound Street, aged 73 years. Her husband was a hackler, a person who separated the coarse part of flax with a hackle.

It appeared that the deceased had for some time been afflicted with a painful disease and was much confined to her bed. She had accustomed herself of late to go to the chamber window in order to obtain fresh air, and on the night of the 11th September, between 9 and 10 o'clock, it is presumed that in going to the window for the same purpose, she unfortunately unbalanced herself and fell into the street upon the pavement and received some very severe contusions, from the effects of which she ultimately expired. Medical assistance was rapidly procured but all efforts to restore animation proved unavailing. Verdict, "Accidental Death."

Most drownings occurred in the summer months when young men took it upon themselves to cool down in hot weather. But just occasionally, a drowning would occur which was not accidental, as we learn from this sudden death in November 1856.

Suicide by Drowning in the River Gipping
An inquest was held before C. Gross, Esq., at the Queens Head Inn, Stowmarket, on Tuesday last, on the body of John Newby, aged 31, who was found drowned. He was last seen alive on Monday morning, between the hours of five and six o'clock. His body was

found by John Barnard the same morning at about seven o'clock, in the river at the bottom of Abbot's Hall fields. Barnard's attention was attracted by seeing a jacket hanging on a tree near the spot.

According to his evidence before the jury, he looked about the meadow to see if he could discover the person to whom the jacket belonged; he then looked into the river and saw a body in an upright position. The crown of the head was just above the water, the hair was floating on the water, the feet lying in the mud – leaving no doubt that the poor fellow had taken off his jacket and jumped at once into the river. No evidence was given to show the cause of the act. He was spoken to by several persons during the previous Sunday and, according to the testimony of his brother-in-law (Mr. Martin), appeared unwell and rather low in spirits, but said nothing to lead one to imagine that he meditated on his self-destruction. He was servant to John G. Hart, Esq., for several years and bore an excellent character for sobriety and industry.

A circumstance was mentioned to the jury that occurred to deceased about seven years since, showing that he had been in an insane state for upwards of four hours, had walked during that time about 15 miles, and had not known where he had been. Therefore the verdict arrived at was: "That he had committed suicide by drowning, whilst in an insane state of mind."

The danger of handling loaded firearms still posed a problem with a number of incidents, some of which resulted in sudden and immediate death. This next sudden death at Butley was typical of that type of accident.

Fatal Gunshot Blast

An inquest was held by Mr. Wood, Coroner, on the 7th November, at Butley Mills, on the body of Pells Watson, aged 19 years. A heron had frequented the mill dam and Watson had, in the afternoon of the 5th, loaded a fowling piece for the purpose of shooting this bird on his next visit. The following afternoon a quantity of rooks were flying past the windmill and Watson told his fellow miller he would have a shot at them and went to fetch the gun. In reaching down over a flour-bin for the gun, it went off and the whole contents, lodging under his right arm, killed him on the spot. Verdict, "Accidental Death." Mr. Sewell gave Watson a most excellent character and it is much to be lamented that he came to such an untimely end.

Trapped Between Millstones

We might find it difficult to imagine that a ten year old boy could be left alone in an operating windmill but this was the case at Wickham Skeith in December, resulting in another tragedy. The fatal accident resulted in the death of a lad named Arthur Whitmore, about 10 years of age, son of Mr. Robert Whitmore, miller. His father left him in the mill whilst he went to breakfast, having directed him to put the corn forward to the hopper, but cautioning him not to go near the wheels.

Another boy was in the mill, and it appears that Whitmore was showing the lad how the machinery worked, when his clothes became entangled, and he was drawn between the cog wheels to the spout which feeds the stones. He was whirled round with the spindle several times, and part of his body was literally jammed between the stones, presenting a most pitiable object. The other lad had a narrow escape, for in endeavouring to extricate his companion, his thumb was so bruised as only to hang by a piece of skin. An inquest was held on Monday at Wickham Swan, where the jury returned a verdict of "Accidental Death." This accident should operate as a caution to millers not to leave machinery so exposed.

So ended the year 1856 – a remarkable year for sudden deaths but a year which was about to be matched by a veritable cornucopia of sudden deaths, many of which were entirely preventable. Before we read of the year 1857, we shall read a few lines about the coroners of Suffolk who carried out their duties in all weathers to all the corners of the county.

A Word About Coroners

Gross, Jackaman, Marriott, Wayman, Wood. These were the surnames of coroners that we read about who presided over many of the inquests in Suffolk during the early years of Queen Victoria's reign. We read little about the coroners themselves so perhaps at this juncture, we should examine the working lives of our County Coroners. What were the boundaries of their responsibilities and how did they get appointed?

Suffolk had two coroners for the county – the County Coroner and his Deputy. Their domain of responsibility was not limited. Thus in 1861, Frederick B. Marriott, based in Stowmarket, was the County Coroner and Walter B. Ross was the Deputy Coroner, based in Ipswich. However, there were two Liberties in Suffolk – the Liberty of St Edmund (West Suffolk) and the Liberty of St. Etheldreda (much of East Suffolk) and each Liberty had its own coroner.

The Borough of Ipswich also had its own coroner – Simon B. Jackaman Esq. In addition we should not omit to mention the coroner for the Liberty of His Grace the Duke of Norfolk, a large area which straddled parts of south Norfolk and north Suffolk.

So, all in all, there were at least six gentlemen carrying out their responsibilities as coroners in the county.

The coroners for the Liberties were appointed by the Crown via the chief steward of each Liberty whereas the County Coroner was elected by the freeholders of the county– that is, anyone who owned unencumbered freehold land within the county. The freeholders who would vote usually numbered about two and a half thousand votes. The County Coroner was, once elected, in the position for the rest of his active life. The coroners were professional men, usually solicitors, and they might also be involved in some administrative functions, such as being the Clerk to the Board of Guardians of a Union. They might also be serving churchwardens or landed estate agents.

An election was actually an exciting affair though the majority of the general public showed little interest in the goings-on at Ipswich Town Hall, where the voting took place. The election would usuually come down to a choice of two candidates who canvassed for the support of each freeholder. The election was, on the face of it, a non-political event but it usually came down to a choice of a Conservative and a Radical candidate.

Both candidates would try to ensure that their voters reached the Town Hall in good time to cast their votes. A convoy of carts might have made the arduous journey from one area of Suffolk to vote for their man on the appointed day at Ipswich. It appears from the newspaper report of an election that a running count of the voting was kept and the situation would swing in favour of one or the other candidate in just a matter of hours until late in the day, a final result was pronounced.

We will now briefly look at some of the personal circumstances of the coroners. We begin with the Coroner for the Liberty of St. Etheldreda. This was Cooper Charles Brooke (1816-1896), solicitor, who lived at The Mount, Woodbridge and was appointed Coroner in 1858. He succeeded John Wood Jnr. who died in office. It was said that the position of coroner had been held by the Wood family for many years. In Brooke's period in office, of about thirty years, no less than 1,580 inquests were held in the Liberty. This equates to about one inquest per week. His son Walter became Deputy Coroner in 1887, perhaps with a view to succeeding his father at the appropriate time.

Travelling westwards and we enter the jurisdiction of the Liberty of St. Edmund for which Harry Wayman (d. 1861) and George Anthony Partridge were the successive coroners during our period of study. Partridge worked as a solicitor out of his offices at 17 Westgate Street, Bury St. Edmunds. Harry Wayman had also lived and worked as a solicitor in the centre of the town.

In the 1850s, the coroner for the Liberty of His Grace the Duke of Norfolk was attorney-at-law Charles Gross, who lived at Colman Villas on Norwich Road in Ipswich, close to St. Matthews church. His area of responsibility consisted of a broad swathe of central Suffolk from Samford Hundred in the south to Hartismere Hundred in the north with the Hoxne and Blything Hundreds to the north-east. His duties must have involved a great deal of travelling on both the Ipswich Turnpike and the Ipswich-Norwich road (now the A140). In 1859, his role as coroner was taken by his son Benjamin and a deputy coroner for this Liberty was also appointed.

In the Borough of Ipswich, the role of coroner had been held by the Jackaman family since at least 1800 when it was reported that Simon Jackaman had been elected coroner by the Corporation at a Great Court held in the Moot Hall. His son Simon Batley Jackaman was elected coroner for the Borough in 1823 and he held the position for fifty years before retiring in 1873. His son Henry Jackaman was then elected. The Jackaman firm of solicitors still practises in Ipswich and other towns to this day.

All of these men were honourable public servants who gave great service to their county. This was never more amply described than in the newspaper obituary of Simon B. Jackaman in 1875, a few lines of which are reproduced here. "To his juries, witnesses, to public officers, and to all concerned in the gruesome business of holding inquests, Mr. Jackaman was a model of patience and kindness. His care in avoiding all that might wound the feelings of the bereaved people who necessarily came before him was dictated by his native benevolence of heart. No child or widow ever needed to hesitate in telling their mournful tale to him, and his kindness and consideration under painful circumstances are well remembered in many a humble home in this town."

Simon Batley Jackaman is commemorated in a stained glass window (the Good Samaritan window) in the church of St. Nicholas, Ipswich. An appropriate family memorial perhaps and also appropriate to the memory of all the coroners of Suffolk who, like the Good Samaritan, travelled great distances to help their fellow man.

1857

"Nothing ever happens here." For many quiet Suffolk parishes, this would be a familiar answer to the enquiry made by the passing stranger to the village rustic. Month after month would go by without the slightest disturbance to the agricultural equilibrium and then a sudden death in suspicious circumstances would have the whole parish chattering. 1857 began like any other year for the coroners of Suffolk, who had to travel far and wide to learn of the extraordinary happenings in otherwise forgotten backwaters.

The Visitation of God at Benhall
An inquisition took place before Mr. John Wood, Coroner, on Thursday last, at Benhall, on the body of Mrs. Ann Christian Smith, the wife of the Rev. Isaac Smith, doing temporary duty there. On Wednesday, Mrs. Smith had been for a walk in the village, and about half past twelve had reached the parsonage lawn on her way home. William Capon, a gamekeeper, was in the adjoining lane and heard three screams; upon looking through the hedge, he saw the lady sitting on the grass and ran to her immediately. Mrs. Bloomfield did the same and they arrived only in time to hear her say, "Oh dear, I am dying," and she actually died before they could get her into the house. Verdict, "Natural

Death by the Visitation of God." Mr. Smith has been a missionary, and with his wife had spent many years in Africa.

Incinerated by Fire in Bury St Edmunds

In January, one Wednesday afternoon, about half-past 3 o'clock, a poor idiot named Robert Pearson, aged 45, who resided with his brother William Pearson, at No. 43, Risbygate Street, was burnt to death. It appears that the deceased, who was a quiet, harmless creature, was left alone for about half an hour, while his brother went to the market; and during his absence, it is supposed, he left his chair and went near the fire, when the fustian smock frock he usually wore, was, by the draught of the chimney, drawn to the fire and ignited. His knees, chest, neck, head and hands were literally burnt to a cinder. He was quite dead when found by his brother, suffocation having no doubt speedily relieved him from his torments. A coroner's inquest was held on Thursday morning, and a verdict of "Accidental Death" agreed upon.

Melancholy and Fatal Accident at Harkstead

During February, an inquest was held at the Rose Inn, Harkstead, before J.E. Sparrowe, Esq., Coroner, upon the body of a boy 11 years of age, named Robert Evans, who met with his death under the following circumstances.

It appeared that, on Friday last, the deceased, accompanied by his father, who is a rat-catcher living in Holbrook, went to Mr. Wrinch's stackyard at Harkstead, for the purpose of destroying rats. Deceased went up a ladder on a stack, in the top of which he put a ferret, his father turning another in a little lower down. In a short time, the father saw a rat coming out of the stack and said, "There comes one," at the same time running towards it with the gun in his hand, when it suddenly went off, and the greater part of the charge entered the right side of the deceased, who at the time was on the ladder watching his ferrets. He stepped about three staves down the ladder and then fell to the ground, crying out, "Oh! Dear!" "Oh! Dear!" The father exclaimed, "I must have shot my boy," and ran up to him overwhelmed with grief. Deceased could not speak but gasped twice and expired. He was then removed home in a tumbril.

At the inquest, the father stated that he believed his hand was upon the trigger, but as he was running at the time he could not say whether he pulled it or not; it was on the cock. The evidence left no doubt that the occurrence was entirely an accident and the Jury immediately returned a verdict of "Accidental Death."

Worse for Liquor in Brundish
An inquest was held at the Crown Inn, Brundish on Monday last, upon the body of Mr. William Golby, bricklayer, of that parish, who died from the effects of an accident he met with on the night of Thursday, the 19th February. It appeared from the evidence that on the day in question, about noon, deceased went to the Royal Oak public house at Laxfield and remained there till seven o'clock, having in the interval had a good deal to drink. Upon his leaving, being worse for liquor, the landlord directed his man to accompany the deceased part of his way home, he having a young pony to drive.

When the man left him the deceased took the reins, and drove on steadily; but he was soon afterwards capsized in a ditch, near the residence of Mr. William Scoggins, by whom he was assisted out and afterwards driven a mile and half towards the Brundish Crown, whither deceased said he was going. Mr. Scoggins then asked if he should go any further with him. Deceased replied, "No,

I think I can drive home now;" and he was then left. About an hour afterwards, as Mrs. Sherman, the wife of a labourer, was passing through Brundish Street, she fell over a person, who proved to be Golby, lying in the road. He said he had been thrown out of his cart and had been run over. He lay across the road, so that a vehicle passing must have gone over his head. Mrs. Sherman ran for her husband, who, assisted by some other persons, put the deceased into a tumbril and removed him home.

Mr. Gooch, surgeon, Stradbroke, was sent for and on his arriving, he found the deceased quite insensible. His body was cold, his pulse feeble and slow, and breathing very much oppressed. Upon removing the dirt and blood he discovered a severe contusion on the orbit of the left eye and temple, and a lacerated wound on the left ear. Mr. Gooch administered the necessary treatment and remained with deceased all night and during the next day. In the evening he was called away and before his next visit deceased had expired. The contents of the stomach evidenced that he had been drinking considerably, the first vomit producing not less than three or four pints of beer mixed with spirits.

Labourer Drowned at Bawdsey
In March at Bawdsey, an inquest was held on the body of James Denny, a labourer aged 38 years. Denny had been subject to fits and had several times been in Nacton Union House, from which he had been discharged about a month. Last Sunday afternoon, being too late for church, he left his sister's cottage, telling her he would take a walk on to the beach, and was not again seen alive.

The following afternoon he was found dead upon the beach by two woman picking up coprolite, his body having been left there by the receding of the sea. It was supposed that, while walking on the Flats at low tide, he was taken in a fit and fell into a hole, out of which he was washed by the very heavy sea the following day. Verdict: "Found Drowned."

Boy Burnt at Sweffling
Another calamitous event and the report of an inquest informs us that boys as young as seven were being employed in the fields when they should have been at school. The inquest was held on March 30th at Sweffling, on the body of John Symonds, aged seven years, only child of John Symonds, of that parish, labourer. This boy had been all day at work with his father. Returning home with both parents about 7 o'clock, he sat down close by the fire. His mother first went out to the village shop and then the father into his master's yard, which was close by, both parents returning about the same time, and meeting this little fellow at the cottage door all in flames.

The fire was extinguished as speedily as possible and Mr. Freeman was sent for, but the poor child died early the following morning. The child sat very close to the grate and he was not aware that his dress was on fire until the flames broke out and as he ran out of the door, the fire increased. The verdict of the jury was "Death from being accidentally burnt."

Brickyard Death at Yoxford
A fatal accident occurred in a brick-yard at Yoxford to a lad named Adolphus Watling, 14 years of age, who was engaged at the time in filling one of the mills with earth. It appears that the pole or shaft to which the horse was attached had to pass over, and within two inches of the frame-work of the mill. The boy had filled the mill, and incautiously laid his arm upon the frame and rested his head on his arm, with his back to the horse, and did not perceive his

dangerous position until the shaft struck the back part of his head. He was heard to cry out immediately when the horse was stopped; but it was too late, the skull of the poor boy being frightfully fractured, causing almost instantaneous death. At the inquest a verdict of "Accidental Death" was returned.

Three Children Dead in June

On the 26th June, at Ousden, on the body of Henry Everitt, aged four years. Susan Everitt, the mother of the deceased, said that deceased was playing about whilst she was cleaning her house and had not been missed by her; but on going to a pond in her garden for a pail of water, she found the child there dead. There are steps down to the pond and a gate, which is usually shut. Verdict: "Accidentally drowned."

On the same day at Clare, on the body of George Nathan Ager, aged four and a half years, who, being left by his mother on Monday the 11th May for a short time, had upset a kettle of boiling water which she left on the hob, and was severely scalded. He died on Thursday week following. Verdict: "Accidentally Burnt."

On the 1st at Keddington, on the body of Maria Cornwell, aged five years. Harriett Cornwell, the mother, said that about a month since deceased had suffered from choking in consequence of swallowing some peas, but she thought had quite recovered. She did not observe any difference in her till last Saturday when the choking again came on. Mr. Simpson, surgeon, made a post mortem examination; the right lung was much diseased, and on opening the bronchial tube, he found a pea firmly embedded there, entirely stopping the passage of air to the left lung, which in conjunction with the diseased right lung he considered had caused the sudden death. Verdict: "Accidentally choked."

Gun Death at Great Bealings
On Saturday June 27th at Great Bealings, on the body of Elvina Hewitt, aged twelve years, daughter of Mr. Hewitt, bricklayer, of Curtain Road, Shoreditch. Hewitt's wife had been stopping at her father's at Great Bealings as she had been in very bad health, and his wife having died the previous week, her husband came up to Suffolk and buried her on Thursday 25th, bringing his daughter with him.

On Saturday last he amused himself by shooting small birds off the cherry tree, with a borrowed gun, and about three that afternoon he and his brother-in-law went down to the river to bathe and on his way hid the gun in a ditch. Before they had reached the river, the report of a gun was heard. The father ran in the direction of the report and saw his daughter fall down. Mr. Acton was sent for but she died in less than ten minutes.

The inference was that the gun went off by accident while the girl was pulling it out of the ditch, and the whole charge lodged in her right shoulder. It is hardly necessary to add that the poor girl was dead long before the doctor could get to the cottage. Verdict: "Accidental death."

Skewered on a Fork
Also in July, an inquest was held at Bredfield on the body of Edward Seammen, aged 12 years, son of Charles Seammen, of the same place, farmer. It transpired that this boy went with two of his father's labourers into the fields to fetch some tares, and was in the cart assisting to load the same. When the horse moved on, this poor boy fell off, and the fork which he held in his hand ran into his throat, causing his immediate death, for he never spoke or stirred afterwards. Verdict: "Accidental Death."

Death from Burning in Ipswich
In November there was another instance of death from burning. The inquest was held at the Half Moon and Star public house in St. Matthew's, Ipswich before Simon B. Jackaman, Esq., upon the body of a child, three years old, named Elizabeth Fuller, daughter of William Fuller, a private in the 15th Hussars.

On the previous afternoon, about five o'clock, the mother of the deceased, after lighting a fire in her cottage, left to get a loaf of bread. Deceased said "I will go too," and her mother expected she was following her; but on Mrs. Fuller getting to the Canteen, which is about two minutes walk from her cottage, she heard screams, and immediately ran back. She found deceased outside the cottage with her clothes on fire. The mother tore them off and discovered the child to be severely burned about the stomach, neck and head; but the little sufferer gave no account as to how her clothes had become ignited.

A man named William Banyard was in the tap-yard of the Half-Moon and Star, when he saw a great deal of smoke issuing from Fuller's cottage and, on going in, he found the deceased lying on the bed, with her clothes on fire, and her hair blazing. He got her up and took her outside, when the mother came up, as stated above. There was no one in the house at the time but deceased and another infant. The poor child was taken to Mr. W. H. Meadows, surgeon, but notwithstanding the exertions used, she gradually sank and died on the following day. Verdict: "Death from Accidental Burning."

Dreadfully Burnt at Hundon
On the 17th December, an inquest was held at the Lion Inn, Hundon, on the body of Ambrose Osborne aged six years. Juliana,

wife of William Osborne, labourer, said the deceased was their eldest child. On the previous Sunday afternoon, she and her husband went to chapel, leaving the deceased in the charge of old Mrs. Childs, who was obliged to leave the house for a few minutes. Whilst she was gone, the child caught fire. Witness heard the alarm and ran out of the chapel. Mr. Nazer, surgeon, said that on Sunday he found the deceased very much burnt about the legs, thighs and abdomen. The child lived till Tuesday morning, when it died from the shock to the nervous system. Several of the Jury were present and helped to put the fire out. Verdict: "Accidentally burnt."

Thus ended the year 1857. One should bear in mind that many other inquests took place during the year. Some of the examples of sudden deaths recalled here and the descriptions of child labour in the countryside cast a light on the very different world that children lived in at the time. It was a world where health and safety were of little concern; where life was one long struggle and where the belief in God's will was reason enough to explain the misery and misfortune that had been inflicted upon oneself and one's neighbour.

1858

Apart from the agricultural accidents and occasional household tragedy, 1858 was a year of low incidence for bizarre and curious sudden deaths in Suffolk. The first sudden death reproduced here was hardly sensational but in the detail of the report, we cannot but notice that a very young boy was required to give evidence; a frightening experience, no doubt.

Fell Through Ice at Lawshall

On the 4th January at the Crown Inn, Lawshall, an inquest was held into the death of Charles Good, a boy of ten years. From the evidence of George Meakin, a child nine years of age, it appeared that the deceased had asked the witness to accompany him to Mr. Moore's pond in a meadow adjoining Lawshall, to see if the ice would bear. Deceased then got on the ice which broke under him and he fell in. Witness ran for assistance but it was an hour before the deceased was pulled out. Verdict: "Accidentally drowned."

Inquest at the County Gaol

A young man named James Turtill died in the Ipswich County Gaol in April and in conformity with a provision of the law, an inquest was held on the same day before B. L. Gross, Esq., Deputy-Coroner. The deceased, who was only 20 years of age, was a labourer from Witnesham; he was convicted at the last July sessions at Woodbridge of fowl-stealing and sentenced to 12 months imprisonment. He was removed to the infirmary on the 4th April, having been poorly a day or two before; he subsequently became gradually worse until his life was despaired of, but on Friday 9th he rallied, got better and more cheerful, so much so that hopes were entertained of his ultimate recovery.

He continued in a convalescent state until Tuesday morning, when he had a change of bed linen and was washed. He afterwards said "I feel comfortable now," and asked for his handkerchief, upon which without a struggle or a sigh or exhibiting the least signs of a change, he expired. His complaint was fever, and during his illness he had been under the constant attendance of Mr. Bartlett, the gaol surgeon, and received every attention from the governor and nurses that could possibly be bestowed upon him. A verdict of "Death from natural causes" was returned. As proof of the excellence of the system pursued in this gaol, it is gratifying to state that it is more than three years since a death occurred there, although in the interval as many as from 1,300 to 1,400 prisoners have been confined within its walls.

Suffered from Severe Diarrhoea

In September, an inquest was held in Ipswich before S.B. Jackaman, Esq., Coroner, at the Crystal Ale Stores, St. Nicholas, on the body of Charlotte Hughes, the wife of Edmund Hughes, porter of St. James's Street. It appeared that deceased, whose age was 39 years, had for a fortnight been suffering severely from diarrhoea, of which she died early on Tuesday morning of 21st. She appeared to have been frightfully neglected, no medical man having been called to her aid, nor anything given to relieve her, with the exception of some porter! No one lived in the house with her except her husband, who, in his evidence, said he did not consider her dangerously ill, or he should have gone for Mr. Elliston, as he once or twice offered to do, but deceased declined, saying she should be better in the morning.

Mr. Elliston, who was called in too late to render any assistance, said he had been the medical attendant for the deceased for the last ten years. He last attended her in January in the present year. She was certainly not a strong woman. He had made a careful external examination of her body, and from its emaciated appearance, combined with the evidence of the husband as to her having suffered from diarrhoea for the last fortnight, his (witness's) opinion was that she died from exhaustion.

If she had had early advice and medicine, the probability was that her life would have been saved. Porter was one of the worst things she could take. He had known the husband for many years and had always found him kind and attentive to his wife; and he thought the neglect he had shown her in the present instance, must be owing to ignorance of her real state. The Jury returned a verdict "that deceased died from exhaustion from continued diarrhoea for fourteen days, without medical aid."

Shocking Death from Burning

An inquest was held at Peasenhall on Tuesday November 30th, before J.E. Sparrowe, Esq., on the body of George Hurren, aged 2 years and 10 months, the son of a bricklayer, of that parish, who came to his death under the following circumstances. On Saturday afternoon the child's mother left the house to go to the shop, a short distance off, to get some butter, leaving the deceased alone in the back room in his night clothes before the fire. The mother had not been absent more than a minute or two when Mrs. Brownsell, a neighbour, was alarmed by the cries of the poor child and, on going into the house, she saw him running from the back into the front room, his night clothes being in flames. She at once took steps to put out the fire but found the child very much burnt about the legs, hands and lower part of the body.

The mother returned home a few minutes afterwards and was greatly distressed to find what had occurred. Mr. Lay was sent for and every attention paid to the little sufferer who lingered until the following day, when he died. The Coroner, though unwilling to add to the grief of the bereaved mother, could not help expressing his opinion that she had been guilty of great neglect in leaving the child in the manner in which she did, and that the circumstances almost warranted a serious charge being preferred against her. The jury, however, looking to the good character which the woman bore in the village, took a more favourable view of the case and, although considering she had shown great want of caution, returned a verdict of "Accidental Death."

In that final paragraph, we read of the "favourable view" of local people to one of their own when severe censure, possible criminal charges and widespread publicity were required to highlight the continuing issue of the misguided neglect of young children. Many more children would perish from burning before there was a realisation from government and local authorities that legislation was needed to protect children from parental neglect in the home.

1859

1859 turned out to be a year in which a number of different cases of suicide took up the column inches of the newspapers. The year itself began quietly for the county coroners but, as winter gave way to spring, an unusual turn of events occurred in Burgate which claimed the life of a farmer's wife.

Set Ablaze by Hot Tar
Before S.B. Jackaman, Esq., Coroner, an inquest was held at Burgate, near Botesdale, on Tuesday April 26th, on the body of Maria, the wife of Mr. Thomas White, farmer, of the former parish, who met with her death under the following distressing circumstances. It appeared that the deceased, who was a fine woman, aged 39 years, was standing by the fire in the back kitchen of her house. Upon the stove was a pot of boiling tar, and her son, George White, was attending to it. Whilst talking to him, a short distance from the fire, the tar boiled over and, running in a blaze along the floor, ignited her clothes.

Instead of throwing herself down, the unfortunate woman ran in an agitated state into the yard, thence through the stack yard into a meadow, where she rolled over into a ditch. She was quickly followed by her husband and son, who, by throwing water over her, succeeded in extinguishing the flames, but not until the poor creature had been shockingly burnt in various parts of her body. Everything was done for her which could be done, but without avail. She died on the following day. Verdict, "Death from accidental burning."

Train Accident near Needham Market
Another young boy fell victim to the railway network in May when a fatal accident occurred one Monday afternoon on the railway about half a mile from Needham station. A lad named Powling, about 14 years of age, was employed keeping sheep. At the request of a labourer who was at work mending the fence near the line, he crossed over the rails with some tools for another labourer.

As he was returning to re-cross the rails, he observed a goods train coming from Needham and waited until it had passed. He then immediately attempted to cross but before he had done so, an up passenger train, which he had failed to notice, came upon him. We are informed that the buffer of the engine struck him; his death of course was instantaneous. An inquest was held at Needham on Wednesday 23rd May by J.E. Sparrowe, Esq., when a verdict of "Accidental Death" was returned.

Buried in Sandpit
A fatal accident occurred on Thursday, the 19th May, on Friston Hall Farm, to a labouring man of the name of Samuel Markham. Deceased was that day employed filling carts with sand and earth from a pit, when a large quantity of earth suddenly caved in, burying the deceased and also a horse and cart several feet. Men were immediately set to work to dig out the deceased, but it was more than an hour before they succeeded in getting him out; he

then presented a most frightful sight, his bowels and some of his bones protruding through his clothes at his back, his skull fractured and his legs broken in several places. Deceased was a very respectable man, and had worked on the same farm upwards of 50 years, the last twenty-three years being with Mr. Hammond, the present occupier. An inquest was held the following day, when an inspection of the pit was made by the Jury and a verdict of "Accidental death" was returned.

Cut Throat with a Razor

On Tuesday 31st May, before W.B. Jackaman, Esq., Deputy Coroner, an inquest was held at Halesworth, on the body of Mr. Robert Hugman, draper, aged 44 years. It appeared from the evidence that deceased belonged to a family, several members of whom had been insane, and he himself lately had been observed to be in a sad and excited state. He lived quite alone, and on Friday last the neighbours, being unable to make him hear, an entrance was effected when the deceased was found dead in his bedroom with his throat cut and a razor by his side. The Jury returned a verdict "That deceased destroyed himself by cutting his throat, being at the time of unsound mind."

Infant Drowned in a Pond

An inquest was held at Stradbroke, in June, on the body of Arthur Betts, aged 18 months. Deceased, the son of Mr. George Betts, bricklayer, was just able to run about and, unobserved, strayed out and accidentally fell into a garden pond and was drowned. The mother, on missing her child, raised an alarm that it was lost and Lucy Pipe, on going to the pond, saw the child's body floating on the surface. It was taken out immediately, a hot bath was procured, and some brandy and water given, but the child was unable to swallow, it being dead. Verdict, "Accidental death."

Suffocated in a Drain

Before W.B. Jackaman, Esq., Deputy Coroner, another inquest was convened in the parish of Brundish, in May, on the body of a child 15 months old, named Jane Pipe, the daughter of a labourer there. The circumstances of her death were abominable. In the absence of her mother one morning, the child fell into a drain containing filthy matter. The poor babe when taken out was in a dreadful state and notwithstanding the efforts of Mr. Read, surgeon, died from the effects of the suffocations on the next day. Verdict accordingly.

Framlingham Suicide

An inquest was held before C.C. Brooke, Esq., at the Crown and Anchor Inn, in Framlingham, on Saturday 2nd July, on the body of Mr. Robert Mabson, landlord of the Queen's Head Inn, who died from the effects of poison administered under circumstances stated in our Journal of June 25th.

It will be recollected that, on the 23rd of June, he purchased some arsenic, for the purpose, as he stated, of destroying rats, but instead of doing so he mixed it up with some water, drank it and then left his house. It being almost immediately discovered that deceased had taken the arsenic, he was followed and Mr. Jeaffreson, surgeon, was sent for. He administered an emetic and attended deceased up to the time of his death, which took place on Thursday, the 30th June. Deceased had been addicted, at times, to drinking to great excess, from which his mind was enfeebled. Verdict, "Temporary insanity, accelerated by drink."

Plunged into a Waterbutt

Another suicide during July was committed at Stowmarket. The resulting inquest was held at the Queen's Head Inn, Stowmarket, before W. B. Jackaman, Esq., Deputy Coroner, touching the death of Elizabeth Gladwell, aged 53, who committed suicide on a Sunday morning, by plunging into a waterbutt where she was found by her husband. It appeared in evidence that the deceased a few days previous to her death had shown symptoms of insanity, so much so, that it was considered improper to leave her alone. During the Saturday night and until one o'clock on Sunday morning, her husband waited upon her. She then appeared sensible, and said she felt better, and requested her husband to lie down and get a little sleep. He did so, but awoke between 2 and 3 o'clock and missed her from his side.

He commenced a diligent search for her, and went down to the river, suspecting she had thrown herself in, as she had expressed a wish to drown herself the day before. He returned to his house and discovered her body in the waterbutt. The deceased, as if to mislead her husband, threw open the door leading into the street and shut the yard door after her. Mr. Harper, surgeon, was almost immediately on the spot, but she was beyond the reach of his assistance. He expressed it as his firm opinion that deceased was, at the time of her death, insane which was the verdict of the Jury.

Suicide at Earl Stonham

Deputy Coroner W.B. Jackaman, Esq., had, the previous day, been at Earl Stonham, presiding over an inquest on the body of Edward Bull, aged 63, single man, who had been found hanging in a stable. It appeared from the evidence of Edward Bull, farmer, and the nephew of the deceased, that the deceased has been for some time past in an unsound state of mind.

At about 4 o'clock on the Saturday morning, he saw the deceased in his stack yard and spoke to him; he seemed to be in his usual state, but about 15 minutes after, upon going to the stable, he saw the deceased hanging by a plough line made fast to a projection in the wall. He cut the deceased down, and a surgeon was immediately sent for, but life was quite extinct. The Jury returned a verdict that "Deceased committed suicide by hanging, being at the time of unsound mind." It was reported that the inquest had been informed that upwards of sixteen members of the deceased's family had previously destroyed themselves.

Scalded in a Tub

An inquest was held before C.C. Brooke, Esq., Coroner, at Brandeston, on the 23rd August, on the body of Elisha Sawyer, aged 3 years. It appeared that the deceased was, on the previous Thursday, in the back-kitchen of his father's house, in which was a tub nearly full of hot sweetwort. His mother had scarcely left the room when she heard one of her children screaming violently, and on returning saw the deceased in the tub, and another of her children (aged 6 years) was trying, but ineffectually, to get the deceased out. Medical assistance was very quickly obtained, but deceased died the following morning. A verdict of "Accidental Death" was returned.

Death from Drowning at Horham

On the 12th August, an inquest was held at the Dragon Inn, Horham, before J.E. Sparrowe, Esq., Deputy Coroner, on view of the body of Amos Sherman, aged 9 years, the son of a labourer of that parish, who came by his death under the following circumstances.

It appeared that the deceased was in the employ of Mr. Cook, a shoemaker, and was sent to a pond on his premises for a pail of water; having been gone longer than was necessary, a daughter of Cook's was sent after him, who upon going up to the pond saw the deceased's hat floating on the water. An alarm was given, and the deceased was found clinging to the steps of the pond, in seven feet of water, quite dead. The Jury returned a verdict of accidental death and the Coroner requested that a hand-railing should be placed by the steps (which are steeper than usual) to the pond.

Infant in Flames at Woolpit
On the 23rd August, an inquest was held at the Swan Inn, Woolpit, on the body of Emily Ruddock, an infant but three weeks old. It appeared from the evidence that the mother, Emily, the wife of John Ruddock, brickmaker, had given the child into the custody of another daughter, aged four years, whilst she went upstairs. She was shortly called down and found the infant in flames. This occurred on the 29th of July, but the child lingered until the 22nd August when it expired. Verdict, Accidental Death. The jury expressed an opinion that the mother did not exercise proper discretion in giving her deceased infant in charge of her little girl, who was only four years old.

Woodbridge Suicide
Yet another suicide was reported in the summer months of 1859. On the 16th September, at Woodbridge, an inquest was held on the body of Mary Cooper, aged 11 years. It appeared that the deceased had, the previous day, at about 3 o'clock, gone up to the attic to look at the train. A little brother and sister accompanied her. She was seen by a neighbour at the window, which she afterwards shut, and told her brother and sister to go downstairs. A few minutes afterwards an elder sister called the deceased, but got no answer; and on-going again to the attic, she saw the deceased suspended by the neck by a ribbon which she had been wearing. The ribbon was put over the rail at the foot of the bed and tied in a fast knot. Deceased was cut down immediately, but was lifeless. The jury

were quite satisfied it was the deceased's own act, but whether designed or otherwise there was no evidence to show, and a verdict to that effect was returned.

Found in a Ditch in Bedfield

On Wednesday 28th December, at Bedfield, an inquest was convened on the body of Mr. William Aldous, aged 69 years. It appeared that the deceased resided at Bedfield Hall. On Christmas Day, between 3 and 4 o'clock in the afternoon, he called at the house of one of his labourers, where he stopped three quarters of an hour, and left about 4 o'clock. Upon leaving, he said he was going home. The deceased, when not returning home as expected, his son and another person, about six o'clock, went in search of him and on passing through Church Lane (which was the way the deceased must go home), they found a woollen comforter and the hat of the deceased lying a few yards off in the middle of the road.

On further searching, they found the body of the deceased lying in a ditch, in which were two feet of water, the head and face of the deceased being above the water. They immediately raised the deceased, but life was found to be quite extinct. Mr. Edward Sharpin, surgeon, Earl Soham, said the deceased was a man of full habit. He had examined the body and found no marks of violence, and was of the opinion that the deceased had fallen in a fit of apoplexy. Verdict accordingly.

Burnt to a Cinder in Ipswich

On the same day Wednesday 28th, at the Feathers Inn, Saint Matthew's, a jury gazed upon the body of Edward Woodward, who met with his death under the following melancholy circumstances. The deceased, an old man of 85 years of age, had been in the army and was formerly coachman to the late Dykes Alexander, Esq., of this town, but had lately been an inmate of Daundy's Almshouses, Lady Lane, where he lived alone, at his express wish. He had been paralysed for the last 26 years and was frequently subject to fainting fits, which sometimes lasted for two hours at a time.

On Tuesday evening, the person who attended the deceased left him quite safe, with a fire burning in the grate. On going to him again the next morning at about half past 8 o'clock, she found the deceased with his face downwards in the fire place and his chest resting on a chair which had fallen sideways against the fire place. He was quite dead, having been burnt to a cinder. It is supposed that deceased was taken with a fainting fit and fell on the fire shortly after being left by his attendant the previous night, as the front and back doors were left unfastened, which was quite contrary to the deceased's usual custom. Verdict, "Death from Accidental Burning."

Coddenham Burning

Another December inquest was held in the parish of Coddenham, on the body of Arthur Grimwood, aged four years. The deceased, who it appeared was left by his mother at one in the afternoon on December 23rd, in the charge of a little girl who was about 9 years old, was roasting an onion when his clothes caught fire. The little girl immediately ran to a neighbour to acquaint her of it, and the little fellow ran after her all on fire. The flames were speedily extinguished, but the poor child after lingering till Wednesday the 29th, expired. Verdict, "Death from Accidental Burning."

1860

Newspaper inquest reports are a constant source of information about social and economic life in Victorian Suffolk. Take the following report which tells us that a boy of nine years of age was working in a factory in Long Melford. It was not until 1878 that legislation was introduced to make it illegal for children under the age of ten from working in factories.

Melford Factory Death in January
On Friday last, a shocking and fatal accident happened to a boy, named John Joslyn, aged nine years, the son of a chimney sweep, who was employed in Mr. William Richold's cocoa fibre manufactory. It appears that the poor lad went incautiously to one of the crushing cylinders in motion, when his arm was caught by the cylinder, which mutilated it in a frightful manner.

The boy was immediately conveyed home, but all that medical skill could do to relieve the sufferer was of no avail, as he sank under it in a few hours. No blame could be attached to any one, as every precaution against accidents is carefully taken. An inquest was held on Monday, before G.A. Partridge, Esq., at the Lion Inn, when the Jury returned a verdict of "Accidental Death."

Woodbridge Rail Death

The month of January also bore witness to a horrific rail death at Campsea Ash. The inquest was held on the body of Henry John Tillett, aged 14 years, son of Mr. Henry Tillett, of that parish, farmer. It appeared that the deceased, for the last few months, had been acting as booking clerk at the Wickham Market Railway Station. On Saturday evening, the deceased took the tickets of the passengers, leaving the down train which reached the station about 7.40, and it is supposed in crossing the line to look after the parcels by the up train which was just drawing up to the station, he was knocked down by the engine, as the driver felt the engine give a slight jump, and the guard felt the same in the break van.

The guard of the Framlingham train was on the up platform but saw nothing of the deceased. He heard the engine pass over something which sounded like the crushing of bones and, getting his lamp, searched and found deceased with the leading wheel of the van on his neck, his left arm was severed and the body fearfully mutilated. There did not appear any fault with the driver or anyone connected with the line, the signal was right for the train to enter and the driver whistled as usual. Verdict, "Accidental death."

Two cases of young children being burnt to death follow. The circumstances of each accident are harrowing. One wonders how the other children who were witnesses to these awful events were affected by what they saw. Contributory factors which led up to these horrific events were the neglect of the adults involved and the absence of fireguards, which most poor people could not afford.

Child Burnt at Bungay
Another January inquest was held at Bungay, before W.B. Ross, Esq., deputy coroner, on the body of Mary Ann Rudd, aged 4 years. It appears the deceased was left at home with two other children by the mother, with a fire in the grate and no guard on. The eldest child, a girl of ten years old, soon after left the house to go to a neighbour's where she occasionally worked, leaving the other children in the house.

In the course of the morning, the neighbour sent her on an errand when she went home to fetch the deceased to go with her, but on getting there she found the deceased upstairs all on fire. A man who was passing noticed smoke issuing from the upstairs windows. He ran into the house, took hold of the deceased and put out the fire. The bolster was also on fire in the bed in which the other child was lying. A medical man was sent for but the poor little sufferer expired the next morning. Verdict, "Death from being accidentally burnt."

Finningham Death from Burning
On Monday 13th February at Finningham, an inquest was held on the body of an infant named Maria Kerridge, aged nine months. It appeared that the poor child, on Saturday, was left by its mother in the charge of a neighbour named Mrs. Gull, whilst the mother went to Walsham, and Mrs. Gull left the child in a room with a little girl about two and a half years old. There was a fire in the room and no guard was on the bars. Mrs. Gull had only been absent about 10 minutes when she heard a scream, and on running into the house found the deceased in flames on the hearth. They were immediately extinguished, but the poor child was much burned, and died on Sunday morning. The Jury, after commenting

very strongly upon the conduct of Mrs. Gull, in leaving the child alone with a fire, returned a verdict of "Death from burning."

Gun Incident at Alderton

Before C.C. Brooke, Esq., Coroner, an inquest was convened at Alderton in March, investigating the circumstances of the death of Walter Buck, aged 12 years. The deceased was, on the day before, employed keeping rooks off some fresh set corn and he had a gun. It appears that another boy, who was similarly employed, and the deceased were talking together and the deceased said the gun was not loaded and he would fire a cap off. Before doing so, he dropped the gun out of his hand, the stock struck the ground, and the barrel fell on deceased's chest; the gun went off, completely carrying away both the lips and the nose of deceased and blazing out his left eye. From the nature of the wound, Mr. Walker, surgeon, who attended the deceased, thought there must have been small stones of some hard substance in the gun; but he found no shot in the wounds. The poor boy lingered for about five hours and was quite conscious before he expired. Verdict, "Accidental Death."

Child in Tub Death at Thorndon

This March inquest was held before W.B. Ross, Esq., Deputy Coroner, at Thorndon on the body of Albert Hammond, aged two years and eight months, who died from the effects of accidentally falling into a tub containing beer which had just been brewed. A verdict of "Accidental Death" was returned.

Death from Burning at Clopton

An inquest was held, by C.C. Brooke, Esq., Coroner, on the 9th March, at Clopton, on the body of Emma Brown, aged three years. It appeared that the mother of the deceased, the previous Tuesday, had left her for a few minutes, whilst she took a dress to a neighbour, under the same roof, to be made. She had been absent a very short time, when deceased was heard crying, and the next door neighbour, on going to see what the matter was, saw deceased standing close to the door, which had been left open, with her clothes in a blaze. Deceased was much burnt about the right side and legs. Verdict, "Accidental Death."

Saxtead Drowning
Another sudden death took the coroner to Saxtead on the 6th June, where an inquest was held on the body of Susan Potkin, aged seven years. It appeared from the evidence of the deceased's mother, that on Tuesday evening the deceased left the tea table for the purpose of fetching some water in a cup from a pond at the end of the house. The deceased did not return and her mother called out for her but she received no answer. She went in search of the deceased, whom she found floating in the pond.

The mother immediately procured assistance and a neighbour named Goddard pulled the deceased out of the water and carried her into a house nearby. Deceased appeared to breathe and every effort was made to restore animation, but to no avail, the poor child shortly after expiring. Verdict, "Accidentally Drowned." The Jury and the Coroner strongly urged the necessity of replacing a gate which had been blown down at the end of the pond.

Lowestoft Child Drowned in a Tub
One Sunday afternoon during July, a child, about 2 years old, named James Chatten, was found drowned in a keeler of rain water upon his mother's premises in Cumberland Street. An inquest was held on the body on the following Wednesday, before F.B. Marriott, Esq., Coroner, when it appeared in evidence that the mother of the child went to chapel on Sunday afternoon, leaving

him at home with his eleven year old brother and his grandfather and grandmother. The elder boy had been playing with the child in the yard but had gone into the house to see to the fire. He missed the child for about ten minutes and, upon going to look, found him with his head and shoulders in a small tub of water, quite dead.

The tub was set there to catch the rain water and contained about nine inches of water in depth. A piece of a comb which the child had had was at the bottom of the tub and it is presumed that he dropped it in, and in trying to get it, over-balanced himself and fell in. A medical man was at once called in but life was extinct. The Jury returned a verdict of "Accidental death," and impressed upon the mother the necessity of covering up the tub, so as to prevent the recurrence of a similar accident.

Cart Accident at Debenham
Another inquest in July was held at Winston before. C.C. Brooke, Esq., Coroner, on the body of Mr. Noah Simpson, of that place, farmer, who had the previous night fallen out of a cart in which he had been driven home by Mr. James Collins of Debenham.

It appeared that Collins got out of the cart to open the gate leading from the road to deceased's house when for some reason the deceased fell over the back of the seat, which was a moveable one. Deceased lived until the following Thursday night. He was quite sensible although his limbs were paralysed which, by the evidence of Mr. L.W. Moore, of Debenham, was caused by the spine of the deceased being injured. Verdict "Accidental Death."

At the same time, a similar tragedy was enacted at Stradbroke with the subsequent inquest being held in Worlingworth.

Schoolmasters Death at Worlingworth

On Saturday last an inquest was held, at Worlingworth, before W.B. Ross, Esq., Deputy Coroner, on the body of Mr. Silvester Tissington, aged 32, the master of the Free School in that place. Deceased, with his father-in-law, had been on the previous day to Stradbroke, in a horse and cart, to see the rifle practice. After the rifle practice, the men visited the White Hart Inn and when they left the inn, it was late and very dark.

When about to return to Worlingworth, Tissington was in the act of stepping into the cart, when the horse suddenly started forward, throwing deceased backwards, bringing his head into violent contact with the back of the cart, and dislocating the spinal cord. The jury returned a verdict of "Accidental Death." The deceased was highly respected in the village where his death caused deep regret. He left a widow and family to mourn their irreparable loss.

Suicide at East Bergholt

An inquest was held at East Bergholt in July, before F.B. Marriott, Esq., Coroner, on the body of Sarah, the wife of George Harvey, aged 39 years. It appeared that last Sunday morning, deceased got up at between six and seven o'clock and went down stairs, leaving her husband in bed. As she did not return after some time, he got up and went in search of her and found her in the privy with her throat cut; she was asked with what she had done it and in reply pointed to a razor which was lying near her.

Mr. Manning, surgeon, was immediately sent for, and he stated in evidence that he found her with a cut across her throat, three inches wide and four inches deep; that she had divided the wind pipe, the gullet, the blood vessel in front, and everything down to the bone; the bleeding had stopped; that she was quite sensible, but faint, and unable to speak, that he tied a few of the bleeding vessels, and in a short time she *walked* up into her bedroom and lay down; she then became suffocated from accumulation of mucus and blood, and died in about an hour. He had no doubt she was predisposed to melancholy insanity, and that while in such a state, she cut her throat. Evidence was also given of her having twice previously attempting suicide. After some hesitation, a verdict of "Temporary Insanity" was agreed to.

Fatal Accident at Kessingland

In August 1860, a melancholy and fatal accident occurred to James, aged 15, son of Mr. James Woolnough, shopkeeper, of Kessingland. It appears that Mr. Woolnough had an off-hand shop at the neighbouring village of Henstead, to which the youth (accompanied by two younger brothers, of the respective ages of 7 and 5 years) was proceeding in a pony cart, and when about a mile from Kessingland, his hat blew off into what is termed a "spring" ditch. He then alighted, and is supposed to have placed his arm round a rail near an archway, upon which he hung while endeavouring to reach his hat, and having lost his hold, fell into the water, striking his left temple against the brickwork as he descended: this is presumed, from a bruise on the temple. The poor children were too young and too alarmed to render any assistance beyond rending the air with their cries.

The wife of Mr. W.T. Balls, auctioneer, of Lowestoft, was the first to pass, and shortly after a person named Cornish, of Westleton, came up, when Mrs. Balls at once directed his attention to the accident. Cornish immediately endeavoured to render assistance, but could see only the poor boy's hat, which he took out and he then drove off to acquaint the parents. The father and a person named Crowfoot went, with a rake to retrieve the body by the foot, and drew it out from underneath the arch. The body was taken to the Queen's Head, at Kessingland, where every effort (under the direction of Mr. Miller, surgeon, of Wrentham,) was resorted to for the purpose of restoring animation, but without success.

Thatchers Death at Creeting St. Mary
In September, before F.B. Marriott, Esq., Coroner at Creeting St. Mary, an inquest was held on the body of William Grimwood, a thatcher, of Creeting All Saints, aged 73 years. On the 23rd, deceased was thatching a barn at the residence of Rev. G. Dupuis, when a stave in the ladder broke and he fell with great violence to the ground, cutting his head dreadfully and sustaining internal injuries, which caused paralysis of the lower parts of his body. Assistance was at once given to him; he was carried into the barn and Mr. Henry Beck was sent for; that gentleman promptly attended and dressed his wounds, and deceased was removed home where every attention was paid him to the time of his death, which took place the following Saturday. Mr. Beck, with other witnesses attended and gave evidence of the above facts, and a verdict of "Accidental Death" was returned.

Thurston Well Death
Before G.A. Partridge, Esq., Coroner – On the 15th October, at the Victoria Inn, Thurston, on the body of Betsey Goldsmith, aged three years. It appeared that the deceased on Sunday, the 14th, was playing near a well, on the lid of which at last she crept. The lid tipped up and deceased was precipitated into the well, where she was drowned. Verdict, "Accidentally Drowned."

Fatal Accident at Laxfield
An inquest was held on Wednesday last, before W.B. Ross, Esq., at Laxfield, on the body of Japhet Short, aged 13 years. On Monday

morning, the deceased was engaged with others threshing wheat with a steam threshing machine, and whilst carrying up the "chobs" from the dresser to the mouth of the machine, he incautiously stepped across the machine upon a handful of wheat which was lying across the mouth, and his leg went in. The engine was stopped as speedily as possible, and the poor fellow lifted out, but not without leaving a foot and part of his leg in the machine.

Medical assistance was speedily procured, and the remedies applied, but without avail, and the poor fellow died the same afternoon. The Jury returned a verdict of "Accidental Death" at the same time expressing an opinion that boys before they are employed in such work, should be cautioned as to the danger.

Fatal Fall at Occold

An inquest was held on Tuesday 2nd October, before B.L. Gross, Esq., Coroner, at Occold, on the body of James Ship. It appeared that the deceased, who was a labourer in the employ of Mr. Clutton of Occold, was engaged carting clover with two other persons on the 11th September. Deceased was on the top of the clover, about three courses above the waggon, and the horses were standing quite steady, when the deceased suddenly fell off the waggon to the ground upon his head. He was immediately picked up and conveyed home in a tumbril, but it appeared that the bone of the neck was injured and he could not move any of his limbs. The poor fellow lingered until last Saturday morning, the 29th, when he died. Verdict, "Accidental Death."

Tetanus Death at Thorndon

An inquest was held before W.B. Ross, Esq., Deputy Coroner, on Friday the 2nd November at Thorndon, on the body of Syer Brewington aged 11 years. The deceased was in the employ of Mr.

Thomas Moore of that parish, and on the 23rd October was engaged harrowing a field with a person named Robert Taylor. They were walking together when all at once the deceased screamed out and on Taylor turning his head saw the deceased lying on the ground under the harrow, the tooth of which had pierced his leg. Taylor immediately released the deceased who it appeared had just lifted the harrow and must have let it fall upon his leg. The wound was very painful and the deceased went home and his mother dressed it, when the deceased, after dinner, against the wish of his mother, returned to his work, from which he did not get home until six o'clock. The wound bled a great deal when deceased's mother dressed and poulticed it, but he did not go to work again until the following Monday, when the wound was apparently free from inflammation, though he walked lame.

On his return home, he complained of a pain in his neck and throat and went to bed about 12 o'clock complaining also of his jaw being stiff. Mr. Miller, surgeon, Eye, was sent for and attended him, but the jaw became entirely set fast early on Wednesday afternoon and the poor fellow died the next morning. Verdict "Death from tetanus, arising from a wound in the leg accidentally caused by the tooth of a harrow."

Stonham Boy Drowned
A second inquest on Friday 2nd November was held in the parish of Wetheringsett, presided over by W.B. Ross, Deputy Coroner once again, on the body of a boy by the name of Denis Pooley. It appeared that the deceased, who was about 4½ years old, left his mother's house to go to school at about half past 8 o'clock on Thursday morning with other children, and about an hour after, his sister came running home and told her mother that deceased was not at school and was lost. His mother immediately went to a

pond, near to the house, and saw a cap floating on the surface, when she obtained assistance, and after some time the dead body of the deceased was dragged out of the water with a rake.

There was a sliding gate at the top of the steps to the pond, and an apple tree grew on the edge. It is supposed that the deceased got over the gate to get some apples and accidentally fell into the pond. The Jury returned a verdict of "Found Drowned," and they expressed their opinion that the pond was dangerous and that a fence ought to be placed round it. They also thought the apple tree ought to be removed, as it was liable to lead children into danger.

Death from Drinking from a Kettle
An inquest was held before F.B. Marriott, Esq., Coroner, on Monday 26th November, at Southwold, on the body of Jane Jarvis, a child aged 3 years. It appeared that the deceased's father was a fisherman at that place and had several young children, but no wife living. His occupation often took him from home and he had been in the habit of leaving his children in the charge of his son, a lad of 12 years old.

Early on the morning of the 23rd, he went out fishing, and, as usual, left his son in charge of his family. The boy, having made the water boil for breakfast, set the kettle by the fire-side and sat down at the table with his back to the fire, when the deceased put her mouth to the spout of the kettle and drank some of the boiling water. Shortly afterwards, the father came in and everything possible was done for the poor child, but she died the next morning. The Jury returned a verdict of "Accidental Death," but, with the Coroner, expressed to the father their opinion that a boy of 12 was not fit to be left in charge of so young a family and that he was bound to provide some proper person.

Youth Drowned whilst Skating at Sudbury

Another winter accident occurred in the county when it was reported that a fine intelligent lad, aged 12 years, the son of Mr. Charles Ray, of Friars' Street, a member of a large and highly respectable family, was drowned whilst skating with his brother on the River Stour, near the Quay. At the inquest held before the Borough Coroner, W. Dowman, Esq., it was proved from the evidence of several persons that the deceased Charles, with his brother Edwin, went with a companion to amuse themselves by skating on the river, but unfortunately went down instead of up the river, the third lad skating at the Reach.

It is supposed the two brothers either fell into a hole in the ice near the centre of the river or that the ice gave way. Both were submerged, but Edwin managed with great difficulty to crawl on the ice, where he lay quite helpless, while his brother was drawn down the stream, and his body was not recovered till life was quite extinct.

A verdict of "Accidental death by drowning" was returned by the jury. Among those present at the inquest were the Mayor, Mr. J.F.S. Gooday, and the Revds. Steer and Bentley, who suggested that, while the frost lasted, ladders and ropes should be kept in readiness near the river, in case of an accident.

1861

We begin the round-up of unusual sudden deaths in 1861 with an accident that was an inevitable cause of injury and death in the countryside – the dangers inherent in a revolving mill sail. What makes this example more unusual is the fact that the mill could not be stopped and, because of that, a second fatality was only narrowly avoided as the father attempted to rescue his son.

Mill Sail Accident at Ashfield-cum-Thorpe

In February, at Ashfield, Mr. Edgar Emeny, of Framsden, accompanied by his son, went to the mill for some corn. Whilst the miller and Mr Emeny were engaged in the round-house, the boy was directed to go and stand by the horse and it appears that when the lad was passing from the mill to the horse, he was struck on the head by the sail, causing a severe fracture of the skull.

The miller and the father, attracted by his groans, went to his rescue and the father very narrowly escaped a similar fate, the sail nearly grazing his head in the attempt to rescue his son. Mr. Sharpin was in attendance as soon as possible, and dressed the wound, but we are sorry to relate that there is little hope of the poor lad's recovery.

Death from Drinking from a Hot Kettle

A child's death occurred at Rushmere in March through the appalling method of drinking boiling water from the spout of a kettle on the cottage hearth. Was it extreme thirst that tempted the child to drink from the spout of the kettle or simply curiosity? The newspaper report was mercifully brief and just mentioned that the inquest was held at Rushmere, before C.C. Brooke, Esq., Coroner, and that it concerned the body of John Farrow, aged two, whose death arose from "swallowing some steam from a kettle containing boiling water, which he was attempting to drink." A verdict to that effect was returned.

Grocer's Suicide at Needham Market

An inquest was held at Needham Market on March 11th on the body of William Taylor, a grocer, aged 68 years. It appeared that the deceased was a man of very eccentric habits and at times very despondent from domestic differences. On the Monday morning, at 8 o'clock, a relative of deceased, observing the shop was not open, effected an entrance into his bedroom where he found deceased lying on the floor, in a dying state, with a cord tied tightly round his neck. The cord was loosened, and Mr. Pennington, surgeon, was called in, but deceased had died from the effects of the injuries he had received. He had been frequently heard to express a wish to destroy himself. A verdict of "Death from strangulation" was returned.

Blaxhall Threshing Accident

A fatal accident occurred at Blaxhall in April. A threshing machine had been at work on Mr. Rope's farm, in that parish, and the deceased, Mary Ann French, had been occupied on the stage in passing the sheaves to the man feeding. The thrashing having been finished, the deceased, in passing towards the ladder by which she had to descend, fell across the drum and her right leg became firmly fixed between the beaters, in which position she was detained several minutes until the beaters could be separated. The foot and leg to the knee were found to be completely crushed and a portion left in the engine. The poor woman was quite sensible up to the time of her death, which took place four hours afterwards. An inquest was held on the body two days later and a verdict of "Accidental Death" was returned.

Worlingworth Child Drowned

An inquest was convened in May, at Worlingworth, before F.B. Marriott, Esq., Coroner, on the body of Phillip Mutimer, aged three years. On a Sunday morning, this poor little fellow was playing in his father's garden, in which there is a pond. He went and asked for his father's hat, which he put on and went out, and ten minutes afterwards was found in the pond drowned. Every means was used to restore him, but to no purpose.

It is supposed he was playing with the water and fell in. A verdict of "Accidental Death" was returned, the Coroner and Jury expressing their opinion that a gate should be put up to prevent other young children from going down the steps to the water.

Child Burnt at Yaxley

On the 1st June, F.B. Marriott, Esq., Coroner, held an inquest at the Red Lion, Yaxley, on the body of Anna Aldridge, aged 2 years. It appeared that on the 1st of May the mother of the deceased left the child alone in her house for a short time, and on her return found her in flames, which she extinguished. Even though the poor child was so terribly burnt, she lingered until the morning of the 30th May when she expired. Dr. Miller having given evidence, the jury returned a verdict of "Accidental Death."

Child Drowned at Wilby

An inquest was held on Friday May 10th, before F.B. Marriott, Esq., at Wilby, on the body of George Watling, aged 3 years. It appeared from the evidence that, on the previous Tuesday afternoon, deceased was seen playing with his elder sister and a younger child in their father's garden. Soon afterwards the girl was heard to scream out that her little brother was in the pond in the garden. Assistance being promptly rendered, the poor little boy was taken out of the pond, and every means was used to restore animation, but to no purpose.

The little girl stated that she went into the house for a few minutes, leaving deceased in the garden, and upon her return and looking for him, she found him in the pond. Both father and mother were from home at work at the time, and she was left in charge of four younger children. The Coroner and Jury expressed their opinion that these children should not be left in charge of a person so young and that some fence and a gate should be put up to prevent them getting to the pond. Verdict: "Accidentally drowned."

Ipswich Child Burnt to Death

Also in May, an inquest was held before S.B. Jackaman, Esq., Coroner, at the Greyhound Inn, St. Matthew's, on the body of Ann Maria Last, aged 9 years, whose parents reside in Globe Lane. It appeared that the deceased on Tuesday morning, about half past 7 o'clock, was lighting the fire, and at the same time playing with her brother, when her clothes accidentally caught fire. The poor child becoming frightened, ran out of the house, when a neighbour seeing her in flames, threw a pail of water over her and Mr. Malpas, of the Feathers Inn, St. Matthew's, coming up at the time, pulled his coat off and wrapped it round her, and thus extinguished the flames. Some of her clothes were then taken off, and she was found to be dreadfully burned. She was taken to the Hospital by Mr. Malpas, where she lingered until Thursday morning, when she died. The Jury at the inquest returned a verdict, "That the deceased came by her death from her clothes accidentally catching fire."

Drownings at Weybread and Brome
An inquest was held on Friday, the 17th May, at the Queen's Head Inn, Weybread, on the body of Frederick Rush, aged 16 months. It appeared that the poor child had been let out at the back door, while the nurse cleaned a stove. On her going to look for him in four or five minutes, she found him in a ditch of water nearby. He was taken out and attended by Mr. Canler, of Harleston; but the vital spark had fled. Verdict, "Accidentally Drowned."

Another inquest was held on Thursday, the 23rd May, before F.B. Marriott, Esq., at the Swan Inn, Brome, on view of the body of William Ling, aged 12 years. From the evidence it appeared that the deceased had been last seen alive sitting by the side of Mr. Mulley's pond, with a little duck at his side. On being missed the same evening, the pond was dragged and his body was found quite dead. The Jury returned a verdict of "Accidentally Drowned."

Yoxford Sudden Death
In May, the parish of Yoxford was plunged into a gloomy state with the news of the death of their local chemist and druggist. This is what the newspaper had to say. "In the midst of life, we are in death. This has been sadly verified here last week in the very sudden death of our respected neighbour, Mr. William Henry Gough, chemist and druggist. The event took place early on Sunday morning last. Mr. Gough was attending his business in his usual good spirits on Saturday evening and went to bed apparently as well as usual. Towards morning, he became very restless and

breathed heavily; getting worse, Mrs. Gough rose in order to procure assistance when he was suddenly taken in a fit of apoplexy. He died about half past six." The melancholy event threw a gloom over the whole village, for Mr. Gough was noted for his jocular character and was, moreover, a generous hearted man. An inquest was held on the Monday afternoon, at the Tuns Inn, when a verdict in accordance with the facts was returned.

Infant's Fatal Chaff Cutter Death

On Tuesday, the 28th June, an inquest was held before F.B. Marriott, Esq., Coroner, at the Red Lion Inn, Mendham, on view of the body of Benjamin Riches, aged two years and six months, who was killed on the preceding Saturday. This child was a son of the man employed by Mr. Stammers to drive the horses working the farm machinery and he went to the place with his two sisters. While there, he wandered into the harness-house, through which the connecting spindle of the horse-works passes to the chaff cutter, and by some means the poor child's clothes became entangled with the universal joint. As a natural consequence it twisted him round the spindle, striking his head every revolution against the floor. The horses were stopped as quickly as possible, and on being released the poor child was found to be dead. Verdict, "Accidental death."

Dennington Child Drowned

An inquest was held on Monday 27th May at the Queen's Head Inn, Dennington, on the body of a child named Susannah Bloss, aged four years. The evidence was to the effect that the child was playing alone by the side of a pond near its parents' house on Friday evening, and that it slipped in and was drowned. The deceased's sister saw some of the clothes floating on the surface and gave the alarm, after which the pond was dragged and the body found in about six feet of water. Verdict, "Found Drowned."

Hadleigh Fatal Accident in July

A labourer by the name of James Pryke, who was employed by Mr. J. Woodgate, farmer, of Brent Eleigh, met with his death under the following circumstances. It appeared that the deceased, with a fellow labourer, had been to the Hadleigh Railway Station with a load of corn, and were returning, with some coals in the waggon, when they met with a friend of deceased's, and were induced to accompany him to a public house in the town, to partake of refreshment; where, after remaining some considerable time, deceased and his companion became, through the liberality of their friend, in a state of intoxication.

About 5 o'clock in the evening, deceased and his fellow labourer started, with the waggon, homewards; and, on nearing Stone-Street, a short distance out of the town, deceased, resorting to the practice too common amongst waggoners, stopped his horses, and made an attempt to seat himself on the shafts of the waggon; but unfortunately lost his balance, and fell. The horses then started off, and the fore-wheel went over the body of the unfortunate man. His companion, who was lying in the waggon, finding an accident had occurred, stopped the horses, and on getting down found the deceased lying on the ground, with one of the wheels resting on his body; and the horses had to be moved on before he could be extricated from his dreadful situation.

Deceased was immediately removed to the White Hart, where J.T. Muriel, Esq., surgeon, promptly attended; but such was the frightful extent of injury sustained, that he shortly afterwards expired. We understand he has left a wife and seven children. An inquest was held on the body on Thursday last, at the White Hart Inn, before John Greene, Esq., Deputy Coroner, and a respectable jury, when a verdict of "Accidental Death" was recorded.

Suicide at Weybread

An inquest was held on Friday the 26th July, at the Crown Inn, Weybread, before Mr. F.B. Marriott, Coroner, on the body of Anne Church, aged 45 years, housekeeper to Mr. Gosling. It seemed from the evidence that the deceased for some time past had been in a very excited state of mind and had been addicted to drinking. On Tuesday evening she retired to rest about 9 o'clock, and about 12, her master heard her making a noise as if dreaming, when he called to her, and in reply she said "she felt very queer." He remained awake some time listening and then fell asleep.

On going down in the morning, at 5 o'clock, he found the back door open. Deceased was found early that morning by a man named Goddard, in a pond on his premises, floating on the water, having on only her night cap and night dress, and a petticoat tied round her waist, and without shoes or stockings. The Jury returned a verdict of "Temporary Insanity."

Death in Pigs Offal

In September, an inquest was held at Wickham Market, before C.C. Brooke, Esq., Coroner, on the body of George Sawyer, aged 15 months. It appeared that the deceased was, on the previous day, at play in his father's garden, in which was a tub containing offal for pigs; the tub was sunk into the ground, and although covers were on it, they were such as were easily removed. A sister of the deceased, who was at play with him in the garden, missed him, and on calling got no answer. She then went to look for him, and saw his feet just outside the top of the tub; he died almost as soon as he was taken out. The Jury returned a verdict of "Accidental Death" and denounced strongly the dangerous position of the tubs.

Drinking From a Boiling Kettle

An inquest was held at Debenham on Friday 27th September, by C.C. Brooke, Esq., Coroner, on the body of Mary Anne Hunt, aged one year and 8 months. It appeared that on the previous Tuesday, the mother of the deceased was preparing dinner and had only just turned round to get some bread, when the deceased attempted to drink from a kettle standing on the fireplace containing boiled water. The inside of the child's mouth and throat were so much scalded that she died the following day. Verdict accordingly.

Infant Death Under a Cart

Another inquest was held at Cookley, near Halesworth, before B.L. Gross, Esq., Coroner, on the body of Ellen Burrows, the infant daughter of Joseph Burrows, a labourer. Death occurred under the following circumstances. Absalom Stone was driving two horses – one yoked in front of the other – drawing a load of bricks in a tumbril, on the high road to Halesworth and he sat on the front of the tumbril to balance it, as the load was too heavy behind. There were no reins attached to the horses, but only short bridles, or "dutfins" as they are called. As he was passing the house of Joseph Burrows, the horses going slowly or at a "foot-pace," the deceased suddenly ran out from an alley and "plunged on the wheels," which passed over her body "in a moment and before anything could be done."

Stone called to his horses and they stopped immediately. The body of the child was picked up by a neighbour and carried to a house; death occurred immediately. The evidence thus far was given by Stone's mother, and she added, that if her son had been walking at the near side of the horses, which was the proper side for the driver, she did not think he could have seen the deceased soon enough to stop the horses in time to prevent the wheel going over her body. Her son sat on the near shaft, bearing down the front of the tumbril, and was looking towards his house.

Mary Jackson, the wife of a labourer of Cookley, confirmed the evidence of the last witness in every particular and added that Stone was quite sober, and that even if he had been in his proper place he could not have stopped the horses in time to save the deceased.

Elizabeth Burrows, the mother of the deceased, was examined but her evidence was unimportant, as she was not present at the time of the accident. Her daughter had not left her side ten minutes when she was brought back by Mrs. Jackson, having been run over by the cart. The Jury returned a verdict of "Accidental Death" but desired that the Coroner would reprimand Absalom Stone for riding in the tumbril without reins and that the police officer would report him (Stone) to the Justices at the next Petty Sessions.

Ipswich Drowning in September
On Tuesday 3rd, an inquest was held before Mr. Jackaman, at the Blooming Myrtle Inn, St. Clement's, on the body of Walter Birch, a schoolboy of ten years of age, who was drowned on the previous day in the river Orwell. The deceased was the son of Luke Birch, (grinder at the foundry of Messrs. Ransomes and Sims), and lived with his parents in Albian street.

The boy went to bathe in the Orwell on the afternoon of Monday, with his cousin Robert Birch, and another boy; none of the party could swim. They went into the water on the hardway at "Hog

Highland." The deceased made an effort to swim and in doing so got into the channel out of his depth. His head was observed by his comrades to rise three times above the water and then they saw him no more. There were weeds and mud at the place but the boys had frequently been there before and escaped without accident. Information of the melancholy accident was given to Birch's father, who found the body after two hours' search and conveyed it home. The Jury returned a verdict of "Accidentally Drowned."

Fatal Accident at Horham
An inquest was held before F.B. Marriott, Esq., Coroner, on Saturday 19th October, at Horham, on the body of William Boon, aged 50 years, farmer. On the previous Wednesday, deceased and his son were in the stackyard loading a tumbril with straw, deceased being on top of the load standing up. The son, wanting to rake down the load at the side next to the stack, for the purpose of making room for him, spoke to the horse to go forward and almost in the same breath stopped him. Deceased, having lost his balance, fell to the ground, and was so injured that he died the next day. The Jury returned a verdict of "Accidental Death."

Laxfield Husband and Wife Dead
On Monday 7th November, an aged man named Robert Marjoram, who has officiated in Laxfield Church as verger for many years, and who was in good health on the previous day (having attended church twice, and a class in the evening), was seized with violent inflammation of the body, which could not be removed, and from which he died on the Tuesday evening.

About a quarter of an hour before his death, his wife, also an aged person, was attacked with paralysis in her left side, and completely deprived of the use of her arm and leg, and she was also partially deprived of speech. She was immediately taken to bed and she remained there in an unconscious state until Saturday, when she expired, and they were both buried in one grave on Monday last.

What an extraordinary conclusion to the year; a year dominated by the drownings and burnings of many infant children. The cottage hearth continued to claim many unfortunate victims and the areas around rural cottages with their deep ponds and streams were an ever-present danger to infants and school-age children alike. This regrettable state of affairs would continue to furnish the newspapers with sensational reports of the misery and misfortune of victims and relatives alike.

1862

The first sudden death reported in the newspapers in 1862 brings a mention of the verdict of "Death by the Visitation of God" which we can remind the reader was a verdict that was used when the cause of death was inexplicable and was attributed to God's will. How ironic, then, that the verdict given at Drinkstone coincided with the man's death inside his church. One wonders what effect this would have had on the rest of the congregation, many of whom would have attended the inquest proceedings.

Death from a Surfeit of Pork and Cabbage

This inquest was held before G.A. Partridge, Esq., Coroner, on the 7th January, at the Cherry Tree public house, Drinkstone, on the body of William Bigsby, aged 51 years. The deceased, an agricultural labourer in the employment of Mr. Whiting, was at church on the Sunday afternoon, and whilst standing up to sing he suddenly fell on his knees and, whilst being taken out, he died. On a post mortem examination by Mr. Leach, it was discovered that the stomach had been gorged with pork and cabbage and that other organs were in a diseased state, death having been caused by the over-gorging of the stomach stopping the action of the heart. Verdict "Died by the Visitation of God."

Death in the Borough Gaol

An inquest was held at the Borough Gaol, before S.B. Jackaman, Esq., Coroner, on the body of Stephen Gladding, aged 35, a prisoner for felony. Deceased, it appeared, had been in the gaol since the 2nd September last year. He had been unwell and had not been able to perform the hard labour to which he was sentenced. He died about half past one o'clock on Saturday morning, after being confined to his bed for about a week, where he was attended daily by Dr. Hammond.

The deceased had not been left alone since Christmas morning and he had been heard to express himself satisfied and grateful for the treatment he had received. He died of typhoid fever brought on by cold and apparently by previous dissipation and distress. He left a widow but no children. The Jury recorded a verdict that the deceased died of typhoid fever and they expressed themselves entirely satisfied that he had been properly and kindly treated in the Gaol.

Fell out of a Cart

An inquest was held at Charsfield on Wednesday 15th January before C.C. Brooke, Esq., Coroner, on the body of John Leggatt, bricklayer, aged 72 years. It appeared that the deceased went to Marlesford the previous Friday afternoon in a cart driven by a man named Sheppard. From there they went to Campsea Ashe and stopped at the Crown Inn in Wickham Market, on their way home. They left Wickham about eleven o'clock at night, intending to return to Charsfield by Pettistree. There were then three people in the cart, the deceased sitting on the near side. On going around a corner in the road leading from the turnpike-road to Pettistree church, deceased fell over the side of the cart and sustained such injuries that he died the following Friday.

After a lengthy investigation, the jury returned a verdict, "That deceased came by his death by accidentally falling from a cart."

Kicked by a Horse at Snape

A fine young man by the name of Daniel Emmerson, a labourer, residing at Snape, and working for Mr. Hambling, was a few days since kicked in the body by one of the farm horses. Mr. Ling, surgeon, was at once called in but he gave no hopes of recovery. Two days after the accident, death put an end of the poor fellow's sufferings. He was a very respectable, inoffensive young man.

The deceased had a brother of the name of Robert Emmerson, in the Artillery, who was engaged with his regiment during the whole of the Crimean War and had escaped "those fearful engagements without a scratch and yet, sad to tell, the poor young man whose untimely end we now record, following a peaceful occupation, came to a violent death. An inquest was held on his body on Monday, before C.C. Brooke, Esq., Coroner, when a verdict of "Accidental Death" was returned.

Mill Sail Fatality at Bedingfield

An inquest was held at Rishangles in January, before F.B. Marriott, Esq., Coroner, on the body of John Flatt, aged 33. It appeared that the deceased went to Mr. Cracknell's mill, at Bedingfield, on Christmas morning, to see a friend, and on leaving he was struck by the mill sail. A man named Osborn heard the mill sail hit the deceased, and ran to his assistance, when he found him lying in a pool of blood, in an insensible state. The mill sails swept within about four feet of the ground.

The mill was not going at full speed, but there was rather more wind when the accident happened than there had been before that day. It appeared from the evidence of Mr Lock, the surgeon, who was called to attend the deceased, that the poor fellow had a contused wound on the right temple, his nose was broken, and his front teeth were loosened. He died the next morning about three o'clock, from the effects of the injuries he had received. Verdict accordingly.

Upsetting a Cup of Boiling Tea
In February an inquest was held by C.C. Brooke, Esq., at Brandeston, on the body of Jane Smith, an infant aged one year. It appeared that one Sunday morning the deceased was standing by the side of the breakfast table, and as her grandmother was pouring some tea, nearly boiling, into one of the cups, the child caught hold of the saucer and overturned the cup, by which she was so scalded in the chest that she died the following day. Verdict "Accidental death."

Sucking a Steaming Kettle
During March, an inquest was held at the Three Cups Inn, Bramford Road, before S.B. Jackaman, Esq., Coroner, on the body of a child 18 months old named Henry Smith. The father William Smith, labourer, resided in Waterloo Street and he had six children, of whom the deceased infant was the youngest.

About noon on the previous day, Ann Smith, mother of the child, was in the front room of the cottage with the deceased and some of the other children. She was making up the fire and the deceased was by her side. On turning her head towards the child, she saw him take his mouth from off the spout of the kettle, which was boiling on the fire. The steam was pouring out of the spout of the kettle. She immediately took the child up and ran across to a neighbour's with him; he was screaming violently.

She had a fender to the fire but no fireguard. It was done in a moment and she thought only the steam passed down the mouth of the child. She took him to Mr. Meadows, who gave him something to ease the burning. The child died at half past 10 o'clock in the evening. A verdict in accordance with the evidence was returned.

Drowned in the River Blyth

Wenhaston was the venue on Thursday April 10th, for an inquest held before B.L. Gross, Esq., Coroner, on the body of William Cleveland, aged 10 years. Deceased was the son of a labourer of that parish. On Tuesday afternoon, at about 4 o'clock, his master, Mr. Robert Bloomfield, farmer, of Wenhaston, saw him sitting by the haystack; he had a dog with him, and was about 100 yards from the stream of water. He was seen afterwards by a little girl, playing with the dog close by the river. He was afterwards missed, and as up to the next morning there were no tidings of him, the waters of the river Blyth were searched, and Aaron Cleveland, grandfather of the boy, found the body at the bottom of the river, about a yard from the bank, in from 5 to 6 feet of water. He could see footsteps on the bank where the boy appeared to have been playing with the dog. From the evidence heard, the Jury returned a verdict of "Accidental Drowning."

Suicide at Melton

An inquest was held, at Melton, on Saturday 26th April, before C.C. Brooke, Esq., Coroner, on the body of Elizabeth Skoulding, wife of Mr. William Skoulding of that place, aged 52 years. Deceased was of a very nervous temperament. She suffered from pains in her head which had lately increased and affected her spirits. On her husband awaking on Sunday morning, at about five o'clock, he discovered that she had left the room. He got up and searched and eventually discovered his wife in a tub of water in the yard, with nothing but her night dress on, and quite dead. The Jury returned a verdict "that deceased drowned herself, being at the time in an unsound state of mind."

Scalding at Wangford

On Monday 25th August, an inquest was held at the Tuns Inn, Rushmere, before F.B. Marriott, Esq., Coroner, on the body of Susannah Briggs, a child two years and three months old, who met with her death at Wangford in the following manner. On the previous Wednesday, the child's mother had been brewing and had taken the first copper of beer off and put it into three keelers outside the back door. Her children had been left in the road but, hearing her child shriek, she ran out and found a neighbour, Mrs. Keeble, had just taken the deceased out of a keeler of boiling beer, into which it had fallen quite up to the armpits. As the beer had not been out five minutes, the poor little thing was dreadfully scalded. It was attended by Mr. Miller, but death put an end to its suffering on the following afternoon. Verdict, "Accidental death."

Another Horham Suicide

The parish of Horham was plunged into a state of melancholy at the end of September with the news that Mr. William Baldry, of the Dragon Inn, Horham, had committed suicide by hanging himself in the wheelwright's shop on his premises.

An inquest was held on Monday 29th, before B.L. Gross, Esq., Coroner, when it appeared that the deceased had been subject to attacks of insanity, and that he was, about four years ago, removed to Melton Asylum, in consequence of one of these attacks. His housekeeper had observed a change in him for the last two months, and although he was rational, he appeared irritable and restless. He had once made an attempt upon his life some years ago, but his housekeeper did not see anything in his condition to lead her to think that he needed to be placed under restraint.

Deceased complained of not feeling well on Saturday, and on Sunday morning said he had not rested well. He ate his breakfast as usual on Sunday morning, and went out for a walk. He did not return as was expected, and a search was made for him, and he was found by his apprentice, lying dead in the wheelwright's shop, with a piece of cord round his neck. The cord had been taken from the turning lathe and, as one end of it remained upon a beam, there is no doubt that the deceased had hanged himself and that the cord broke with his weight. He was a very stout man, weighing about 20 stones. The Jury returned a verdict that the "Deceased destroyed himself while labouring under an attack of temporary insanity."

Fatal Waggon Accident at Bromeswell

An accident which terminated fatally, occurred on Saturday November 8th through the incautious, though not uncommon, act of a man getting out of a waggon whilst it was in motion. The waggon and horses belonged to Mr. Gobbett, of Sudbourne, and had been to Woodbridge. John Meadows, the unfortunate sufferer, and two more men were in charge of two waggons.

On their return homewards, in the parish of Bromeswell, Meadows, on endeavouring to get out of the waggon on to the shaft, fell to the ground, and both the near wheels of the waggon went over his chest, breaking some of his ribs and causing internal wounds, from which he died on the following Monday.

The waggon had in it a ton of oil cake and some coals. An inquest was held at Sudbourne on Wednesday 12th November under the jurisdiction of C.C. Brooke, Esq., Coroner, when, after a long investigation, the Jury returned a verdict of accidental death. The deceased had for some years been in the employ of Mr. Gobbett and was always considered a sober, steady man but was, unfortunately when the accident happened, the worse for drink. He left a widow and six children.

Blaxhall Lad Crushed in Thrashing Machine
On Tuesday last whilst a thrashing machine was at work on Mr. William Hillen's farm at Blaxhall, a lad named Robert Jay got on to the pump of the engine for the purpose of setting a can of oil on the top of the boiler. After he had done so, he turned partly round, and began rubbing the boiler with a rag which he had in his hands, when he slipped and fell between the fly wheel and the boiler. His body was drawn through between them and thrown violently to the ground, and such was the force with which he was carried through, that the rim of the boiler was broken. His death must have been instantaneous. An inquest was held on the body on Wednesday last before C.C. Brooke, Esq., Coroner, when the Jury returned a verdict of "Accidental Death."

1863

The first inquest visited in 1863 was so awful and must have caused much distress for the family and their neighbours. The mother, it seems, did the responsible thing in trying to arrange babysitting for her children and was only absent for a few minutes, which sadly proved fatal for one child.

Death at Earl Soham by Burning

On Friday 30th January, an inquest was held at Earl Soham by C.C. Brooke, Esq., Coroner, on the body of Georgiana Barker, aged four years. It appeared that, on Tuesday the 6th of that month, the mother of the deceased had left her and another little child in her house, whilst she went to a neighbour about twenty yards off, to ask her to take charge of the children whilst she went to Ashfield. She had not been absent more than about three minutes and was standing at her neighbour's door, when she saw the deceased run into the road with her frock on fire. With the assistance of a neighbour, the fire was extinguished but deceased was found much burned. She was attended by Mr. Gross, and lived until the 28th. From the statement made by deceased whilst she was in great pain, it appeared her little sister (about three years old) wanted a stool which she had, and in trying to get it away she pushed deceased on to the fire. The mother of deceased is subject to fits and was in such a sad state as to prevent her being examined. Verdict, "Accidental death from burning."

Two cases of young men drowning follow. The first case resulted from an affliction of the body, the second from an affliction of the heart.

Heveningham Death by Drowning

Just before New Year, a lad named Thomas Kent, 13 years of age, fell into a brook, whilst in a fit, and was drowned. The lad was apprenticed to a shoemaker, living only a few yards from his father's home. In going to his work, he had to cross the brook by a plank bridge, which had a rail on one side only. It is supposed that he was seized by one of the fits while upon the bridge and fell head foremost into the water, for he was found at 9 o'clock on Saturday morning with his head and face covered with muddy, dirty water and was quite dead. His father watched him across the bridge on his way to his work at eight o'clock, but it is probably that he re-crossed the bridge after his father left the spot. An inquest was held on Monday, before B.L. Gross, Esq., and the jury returned a verdict of "Accidentally drowned by falling into the pond whilst in a fit."

Suicide by Drowning at Stanstead

Also in January, an inquest was held at the White Hart Inn at Stanstead, before G.A. Partridge, Esq., Coroner, on the body of James Whiterod, a young man of 19 years of age, who drowned himself in a pond near his father's house. It appeared that the unfortunate young man had formed an acquaintance with a young woman with whom he had hoped to spend the Christmas holidays.

Letters were found upon him from this young woman, declining any further acquaintance, and telling him that she would shut the door upon him if he called and burn his letters if he wrote. This refusal appeared to have preyed upon the mind of the poor lovestruck man, who appears to have been warmly attached to the girl, and he called upon his aunt and a cousin on Saturday, and talked about dying, in a very gloomy, low-spirited manner.

A portrait of the young woman was found amongst the deceased's effects, and a paper enclosed with it containing the words "Dear girl, I dye for you." The jury returned a verdict "That the deceased destroyed himself, but that there is not sufficient evidence as to the state of his mind at the time."

Child Poisoned by Mistake
Finally in January, an inquest was held at the Compasses Inn, Holbrook, before W.B. Ross, Esq., Coroner, on the body of Willie Burrows, an infant, aged 6 weeks. It appeared from the evidence, that the mother and the child were both unwell, and on the Saturday evening, the mother by mistake gave the child some medicine intended for herself. Her own name was written on the label, but the woman was unable to read, and a boy about 11 years of age, the son of the woman, gave his mother a directly opposite message to that given him by the surgeon, Mr. Fleming.

The medicine contained enough opium to kill a much older child than a 6 week old infant. Emetics were given and every attempt was made to keep the child awake but it was found impossible to overcome the effects of the drug and the child died. Dr. Fleming took great pains and gave careful directions to avoid any mistake. The jury returned a verdict of "Accidental Death." They attached no blame to Dr. Fleming, but they expressed their regret that the woman had not been more careful in selecting the medicine and the boy was reprimanded for his carelessness.

Framsden Child Burnt to Death

There was one more noteworthy tragedy to record in the month of January. An inquest was held in the parish of Framsden, before C.C. Brooke, Esq., Coroner, on the body of Emma Woods, aged seven years. It appeared that her mother left her house for a few minutes, leaving deceased with two or three little children younger than herself, for the purpose of assisting a neighbour who was ill. She had not been absent more than five minutes when she saw a great blaze by her own door and on hastening to the spot found her daughter with her clothes a mass of flame. With the help of some neighbours, the flames were extinguished and deceased undressed. She was terribly burnt, but remained sensible till within two or three hours of her death, which took place two days later. She stated that her sleeve caught fire in getting the kettle off the hearth to put some water into her little sister's food. Verdict, "Death from accidental burning."

Suicide at Little Glemham

On Friday, the 6th February, an inquest was held before C.C. Brooke, Esq., Coroner, on the body of Jemima Vale, aged 62 years. It appeared that the deceased had for many years been subject to fits, and was at times very odd in her manner. On Wednesday night she went to bed as well as usual. About four o'clock the following morning her husband spoke to her and she answered him. He then went to sleep again and awoke about half past five; deceased was not then in bed. A search was made for her in the house and garden, but that being fruitless a more extended search was made, and she was found in a pond in the parish of Marlesford, some little distance from her house. The deceased was known to many of the jury and from their personal knowledge of her, coupled with the evidence given, they were unanimously of the opinion that the deceased had drowned herself whilst in an unsound state of mind, and they returned a verdict accordingly.

Tree Fell on Him at Tuddenham

February 1863 saw a visit by the coroner to the parish of Tuddenham because of the following incident. John Wade, 62 years old, was employed with another man named Whitmore, cutting down a large poplar tree on Mr. Neve's farm. After some of the roots had been cut, Whitmore observed the earth round the tree begin to give up and he at once called out to the deceased, who ran away, but unfortunately in the exact direction the tree fell. One of the branches struck him on the back of his head, knocking him down and resting upon his head. His death must have been instantaneous.

The tree was growing in a light sandy soil, and it is supposed the earth gave way in consequence of the purchase the strong wind had on the upper branches and the principal roots towards the wind had been cut through. Whitmore stated he thought there would have been about three hours more work before the tree was felled.

Deceased was a very steady quiet man, and had worked on the same farm for about thirty years. Verdict, "Accidental death from the falling of a tree."

Fatal Gun Accident at Offton
On Thursday, the 12th February, a man named Prentice, in the employ of Mr. Joseph Clarke Kistruck, of Offton, farmer, was alarmed by hearing his master call out, as if in pain and needing help. Prentice immediately went to the end of the front garden, whence the sound proceeded, and found Mr. Kistruck sitting upon the ground with his gunstock lying near him and apparently badly hurt.

Mr. Kistruck was immediately removed, when he then informed Mr. Raynham, a neighbour, that the barrel of his gun fell from the stock as he was walking with it in his hand, and immediately exploded. The nipple of the barrel which exploded was broken and the keep of the gun was in very bad order. Mr. Beck, surgeon, of Needham Market, attended the deceased immediately after the accident, and found that the charge of the gun had passed through the thigh, but without injuring the bone or artery.

Mr. Beck consulted with Mr. Grouse, of Bildeston, and they decided to wait before proceeding to amputate the limb. The shock to the system, however, was so great that the deceased was seized with vomiting which could not be subdued, and he gradually sank and died on Friday afternoon. Deceased, who was much respected, was 46 years of age, and leaves a widow and 12 children. An inquest was held before B.L. Gross, Esq., and the jury returned a verdict of "Accidental Death."

Death from Worms in Blaxhall
During April, an inquest was held at Blaxhall, by C.C. Brooke, Esq., Coroner, on the body of Agnes Levett, aged 8 years, who, while running along the road fell and died in a very few minutes. It appeared she had for some time been subject to worms and

the day before her death one was pulled from her nose, about eight inches long. Mr. Jones, of Woodbridge, surgeon, was of the opinion she had died of convulsions, of which the worms might have been the cause and the jury returned a verdict accordingly.

From the horrifying nature of poor little Agnes's death, we continue onto the more mundane nature of cart accidents which resulted in the death of each carter.

Tannington Accident

On Thursday evening, May 28th, about seven o'clock, as a man named David Leeder was passing through this village, driving a waggon laden with manure, he fell from the shafts and both wheels on the near side of the vehicle passed over him. It appeared that the deceased was seen a short time before the accident by a man named John Wythe, and was at that time standing upon the shafts between the two horses. He appeared at that time to be asleep, and Wythe called out to him. He turned round to Wythe, and asked what he wanted. He was shortly after seen by a man named Woods, a miller, to fall under the wheels on the near side. Woods immediately stopped the horses, and procured assistance.

Deceased was found to be bleeding from the mouth and nose. He was removed to the Tannington Horseshoes Inn, and medical assistance was immediately procured but he was so much injured that he died about half past eleven that night. Deceased who leaves a family of seven children, was about 38 years of age, and was on his way from Diss (where he resided) to

Mr. Cook's of Dennington. An inquest was held upon the body on Saturday, before B.L. Gross, Esq., Coroner, and the jury returned a verdict of "Accidental Death."

Thornham Boy's Cart Death
Another May inquest was held in the parish of Thornham, before F.B. Marriott, Esq., Coroner, on the body of William Copping, who had been killed in the manner detailed by the only witness, Mr. Alfred Cracknell, farmer, who said, - The deceased was in my employ; he was 14 years old. Yesterday, at about noon, when in the road by my house, I saw a horse and tumbril which I knew to be mine, coming at a tremendous pace along the road, and I saw it was the deceased riding sideways on the horse. Directly I saw him he attempted to jump off; he did not clear the wheel of the tumbril, and it went over him. I called Birt, who was working in the garden, and went directly to the deceased. He was in an unconscious state. He was taken to his home and I gave him some brandy and put some vinegar to his lips, and he revived for a time, but died in about an hour after the accident. He was undressed and put to bed, I asked him where the pain was, and he said, "Everywhere, Master." He knew me and his father. There was a slight bruise on his thigh, and I think the wheel must have passed over the middle of his body. The tumbril was empty.

On the previous Wednesday, on my return from Bury, I had found that the same horse had run away in a tumbril, and that the little brother of the deceased, a boy only seven years old, then had charge of it. On the Thursday morning I reprimanded the deceased very severely for letting his brother go with the tumbril, and told him never to take the horse again; and it was contrary to my orders that he took the horse yesterday. He had been carting some oil cake from my farm to an off-hand farm, and was returning with an empty tumbril. The horse ran into my stackyard and catching the gate post turned the tumbril over and broke the shaft. Directly the accident happened, I sent for Mr. Downing, surgeon, of Gislingham, but he did not arrive until after the boy was dead. From the evidence, the Jury returned a verdict of "Accidental Death."

Bloomfield Girl in Beer Tub

An inquest was held at Pettistree on Monday 1st June, before C.C. Brooke, Esq., Coroner, on the body of Ellen Bloomfield, aged 3½ years. Deceased was at play in the yard at the back of her father's house, on Friday, the 29th May, where her mother had put some beer in three small tubs to cool. The mother hearing the deceased scream violently went into the yard and found her lying over the tub with her feet on one side and her head on the other. Her back and left arm were in the beer which was just off the boil. She was quite sensible and said she had fallen in the tub. Mr. Cochrane, of Wickham Market, attended her but the shock to the system was so great that she died on Sunday morning. The verdict arrived at was "Accidental death from falling into scalding beer."

Railway Death at Campsey Ashe

One August morning, a man named Philip Kerridge, 85 years of age, was run down by a train and killed while crossing the line at Campsea Ashe. It appeared that the poor old man left his house at Campsea Ashe that morning with the intention of going to Tunstall to see his daughter, and in doing so, as was his custom, he proceeded to cross the line near the Railway Station. The 6.35 up train from Yarmouth was nearby at the time but the deceased did not appear to see or to hear it. The engine driver saw him when he was nearly on to him and sounded the whistle several times, but it was too late to stop the train. The deceased appeared to take no notice of the whistle and was struck down by the buffers, when his left hand was cut to pieces, and he received such injuries on the head that he died a few minutes after.

An inquest was held on the body upon the same day, at the Talbot Hotel, before C.C. Brooke, Esq., Coroner, when from the evidence it appeared that the accident resulted entirely from the unfortunate <u>deafness</u> of the deceased, and that no blame could be attached to any of the Company's servants, and a verdict to that effect was returned.

Fressingfield Child Burnt to Death
On Saturday 22nd August an inquest was held before B.L. Gross, Esq., Coroner, at Fressingfield on Mary Ann Birch, aged seven years. It appeared that on the previous Tuesday evening (18th), between eight and nine o'clock, the deceased went upstairs to go to bed and her mother left a lighted candle at the top of the stairs. The deceased took the candle afterwards and set it on a chair. Shortly after, the deceased was heard to call out "Father." Her father ran upstairs and found the deceased partly undressed and surrounded by flames; she seemed choked. Her father seized her in his arms and put out the fire, and sent for Mr. Pretty.

The deceased told her father that she had put the candle on the chair and leaned forward to put the blind close to the window, and that her clothes caught fire. Mr. G.W. Pretty, surgeon, of Fressingfield, attended the deceased and found her very extensively burnt about the face, body, arms, and legs. Deceased never rallied from the shock and died from the effects of the burning on the Friday. Verdict: "Accidental Death."

Occold Young Womans Death

In September, an inquest was held at the Bottles Inn, in this parish, before W.B. Ross, Esq., Deputy-Coroner, upon the body of a young woman named Emma Ling. It appeared that the deceased had been living with her brother for the last month, and previously to that she had been in the Eye workhouse.

Her health had been very bad for six or seven years, and during the last week she was worse, not being able to keep up more than two or three hours in the day. She had not had any medical attendance for several months and was last attended by Dr. Miller, of Eye, while she was in the workhouse. Deceased was supported, since she left the workhouse, by her brother, and on the night before her death, she ate a hearty supper and went to bed about 11 o'clock. She was unable to rest and died at half past two on the following morning. Deceased had refused to return to the workhouse and did not appear to have wanted for the necessaries of life at her brother's house. The Jury returned a verdict of "Death from natural causes."

Lavenham Suffocation

Also in September, at Lavenham, as two men were employed in the completion of a well, which they had been deepening for Mr. Mumford at the Hill House, when only about ten minutes' work remained to be done, one of the men, named Geo. Ellis, had to go down a few feet for the purpose of taking some measurement for a little iron-work which was required. It was known that there had been foul air in the well, as the men had discovered it on the previous day, and accordingly it had been left open, that the air might escape. However, the men had been at work before breakfast, and there did not seem to have been more than ordinary danger. The work was completed with the exception of the little matter which Ellis was proceeding to attend to.

After breakfast, and just previous to their intended start for home at Bury, he had descended the ladder about 12½ feet, and reached the wooden stay on which it rested when Mr. Mumford, who was at the mouth of the well, heard him breathing very heavily and, looking down to ascertain if anything was amiss, saw him slip down in a sitting posture between the ladder and the side of the well. His companion, George Jude, was sent down to rescue him, but before he could adjust the rope by which Ellis might be drawn up, he himself was so affected that his life would also have been lost if he had not been immediately drawn up.

Mr. Barkway was at once sent for, and attended to Jude, and advised the "snaring" of Ellis by means of a rope, and bringing him up that way. This was done, but of course his death had been almost instantaneous. Immediate information was forwarded to the Coroner at Bury, and the inquest was held on Wednesday. Verdict: "Accidental death from suffocation, no kind of blame attaching to any person whatever." Ellis was about 54 years of age, and leaves a widow and two grown-up sons.

Threshing Death at Little Thurlow
September also saw an inquest being held at the Cock Inn, in Little Thurlow, before G.A. Partridge, Esq., on the body of Richard Radford, aged 6½ years, who met with his death on Tuesday afternoon, under the following circumstances: - Samuel Reeve, deposed: I manage the threshing machine belonging to Mr. Wm. Chapman, of Kelton Leys. On Tuesday, we were threshing barley at Mr. Bailey's at Little Thurlow. Deceased got up to help me to clear the scaffold on which the corn is put before

it goes down into the machine. We were just finishing our job and I had got my back towards the deceased when we were both sweeping the remains of the corn into the machine. I turned my head and found deceased in the machine. I heard a noise and the strap flew off and the machine broke. I jumped down to unscrew the drum and get him out: he was dead. A great deal of blood was in the machine: one of the deceased's legs was nearly torn off. The scaffold all around the mouth of the machine is perfectly level; it does not incline inwards. I have a hole to stand in myself when I am regularly feeding the machine. The Jury at the inquest returned a verdict of "Accidental death."

Framlingham Cart Death
We move on to October and an inquest held in Framlingham on Friday, the 30th, before C.C. Brooke, Esq., Coroner, on the body of Mr. Charles Hall, of the Steam Mills. It appeared that deceased had, the day before, been to Woodbridge Market, and on his way home called in at about 10 o'clock with Mr. King, at the Willoughby Arms, Parham. After staying a few minutes, the deceased left, driving very steadily; Mr. King left immediately afterwards, and when he got some little distance along the road, he overtook a horse pulling an empty cart. This he found was the deceased's. After releasing the horse, he returned to look for the deceased who was found by a lad named Hurry sitting on the bank near the Broadwater bridge. With assistance, the deceased walked some little distance and was ultimately carried home and attended by Mr. Jeafferson, but died the following day.

There were marks along the road for five or six yards, as if deceased had been drawn along, and the following morning marks were distinctly seen of a wheel having passed over a post standing on the crown of the bridge, also marks of a wheel on the side and top of the wall. The post on the bridge was represented as standing in a very bad position, and the only way the accident could be accounted for was that deceased drove too close to the side of the bridge and accidentally drove against the post; but he was not at any time sufficiently conscious to give an account of it.

From the evidence, it appeared that the deceased was quite sober. Mr. Jeafferson having given medical evidence, the Jury returned the following verdict, "That the death of the deceased was caused by his cart being upset, whereby he was thrown out and died from compression of the brain caused by such a fall." The Jury also strongly recommended that the post which stands very badly on the crown of the bridge should be removed.

Wenhaston Infant Death

An interesting inquest was held at Wenhaston on Monday 16th November before B.L. Gross, Esq., Coroner, on the body of an infant, 10 months old, named Maria Moor. The inquest report is reproduced here word for word.

"Harriet Moor, the mother of the infant, is an unmarried woman, living at Wenhaston with a hawker, named William Tuthill, with whom she has lived for six years. She stated before the Jury that this was her last-born child and that now she had none living. It had been pretty healthy from its birth and had never had medical attendance. On Thursday, the babe was attacked with diarrhoea and she put some light wine in its sop (bread soaked in gravy or soup). The child was, soon after, sick and it died on the Saturday afternoon. Nobody saw the child during its illness except its mother and father, till just before it died on Saturday, when Mrs. Lucy Tuthill saw it. Witness did not send for a medical man as she did not think the child was dangerously ill. She lost one child before at 2 years old and another at six months old; those children were attended by a medical man in the Union.

Frederick Haward, surgeon, of Halesworth, deposed that, on examining the body after death, he found it much emaciated but there was nothing externally that would account for its death. His opinion from the evidence which had been given and the appearance of the child, was that the child died from exhaustion caused by the diarrhoea and that was produced by unsuitable food and nourishment.

The Jury returned a verdict in accordance with the medical evidence and requested the Coroner to express to the mother of the child their opinion of her culpable neglect in not taking proper care of the child and neglecting to apply for medical assistance. The woman was accordingly reprimanded by the Coroner." This was another of those sudden death cases which occurred frequently but did not often feature in the newspapers.

Turnip Machine Death at Witnesham
An inquest was held in the parish of Witnesham on Wednesday the 2nd December, before C.C. Brooke, Esq., on the body of James Smith, aged 9 years. It appeared that on the previous Friday week, the deceased was at work on Mr. Barker's farm putting turnips into a turnip mincer, when the thumb on his right hand became entangled in the machine, and was very much lacerated.

Mr. G.F. Meadows, of Otley, dressed the wound and saw deceased several times afterwards. For the first few days the wound appeared to be healing properly, but mortification afterwards took place, and subsequently lock-jaw, which caused his death on Monday last. The jury returned the following verdict, "That the death of the deceased arose from tetanus, caused by his thumb being accidentally injured in a turnip cutting machine."

1864

As we draw towards the end of this litany of fatal events, we can see how 1864 represents all that was typical of the rural misfortunes suffered by the population. A drowning, a burning, a cart accident involving a young boy and the seeming neglect of an illegitimate child all feature prominently in this period. Yet we begin with one of those instances of natural death which did not always make the newspapers.

Sudden Death from Natural Causes

At the beginning of the year, an inquest was held at the Ship Inn, Carlton Colville, before F.B. Marriott, Esq., Coroner, on the body of Mary Ann Hawkes aged 48. Her husband deposed that during Monday and Tuesday the deceased complained of pain in her back and side; this was worse on Tuesday night. Deceased did not ask for a doctor to attend her. She remained up until midnight, getting her son's things ready as he was going to sea. The witness did not hear her come to bed, but at about five o'clock on Wednesday morning he was awake and deceased complained that he had all the clothes and she was cold. She got out and into bed and about ten minutes after he heard a rattling in her throat; he shook her but she did not speak. Witness got up in the bed and lifted her up in his arms and tried to set her up. He then called to his son to bring a light and on its being brought he saw that she was dead. He went for Mr. Smith who came.

Mr. Smith stated he had examined the body externally and found no unnatural appearance about it. Some five years since, he had attended deceased in an illness when she had symptoms of a diseased heart. He then thought she could never recover. She had complained frequently of palpitation of the heart and he had no hesitation in saying that death resulted from it. The Jury returned a verdict of "Natural Death."

Death from Burning at Lawshall
Later in January an inquest took place at the Swan Inn, Lawshall before Mr. Partridge, Coroner, upon the body of a widow named Alice Rolfe. Deceased, who was 85 years old and very feeble, lived alone in a small house opposite Lawshall Church, but a grand-daughter named Catherine Nunn was in the habit of sleeping with her. On Monday morning she was left between 10 and 11 o'clock quite well but when the grand-daughter returned to the house in the afternoon, she found the deceased quite dead.

Her clothes were almost all burnt off but were not burning when the body was discovered and seemed to have been out for some time. It is conjectured that while sitting by the fire her clothes were accidentally ignited and that in endeavouring to get to the door to give an alarm she fell in consequence of her fright and infirmity, and was unable to get up again. None of her neighbours heard any call for help but it happened that most of them were out for the day, though one saw her safe after dinner. The Jury returned a verdict of "Accidentally Burnt." A second similar case occurred in the parish of Dennington a week later.

Dennington Widow Burnt to Death

An inquest was held at the Queen's Head Inn in this place on Saturday 16th January before E. Lawrence, Esq., Coroner, upon the body of an aged woman named Lydia Emery, who died on the previous Thursday from the effects of severe burns received on Tuesday 5th January. The deceased was 75 years of age and according to the evidence of her husband she got a basin of water to wash his face. She stood washing his face with her back to the fire and her clothes suddenly blazed up. Deceased called out and a neighbour ran in and put some water on her and extinguished the flames. Mr. Grimshaw, surgeon, of Laxfield, attended deceased but she died on Thursday 14th. The evidence of the husband of the deceased was corroborated by that of the neighbours and the Jury returned a verdict of "Death from Accidental Burning."

February Poisoning Case

An inquest and subsequent murder enquiry took place in February on the death of Eliza, the 9 year old daughter of John and Sophia Bootman of the parish of Wissett, the details of which were quite the most traumatic one could imagine. The basic details were that the wife, Sophia, concocted an ointment containing arsenic (used for destroying vermin) and applied said ointment onto her daughter's head which was infested with lice. The outcome of the inquest and trial showed that death was entirely due to the absorption of arsenic through the scalp but that there was no intention of malice on the part of either parent. The Jury were directed to bring a verdict of *homicide per infortunium*, meaning that the deceased died from the effects of an ointment containing arsenic applied to the head of the deceased by one Sophia Bootman, the said Sophia Bootman being ignorant of the effects of such application, and intending thereby to heal a disease of the scalp of the deceased.

The Jury desired the Coroner to express to John and Sophia Bootman their sense of their neglect of the deceased. The Coroner accordingly reprimanded Bootman and his wife, and they were discharged from further attendance.

Another Child Burnt to Death

The inquest at Earl Soham in April into the death of an eighteen month old child, Sarah Harvey, posed a great many questions which were not answered by the newspaper report of the proceedings.

It transpired that on the afternoon of Saturday 23rd April, the mother of the deceased left her with her two brothers, the eldest of which was six years old, for the purpose of going to Framlingham. Before leaving she locked up the house, but left the backhouse unlocked and asked the daughter of a neighbour to keep an eye on the children. Shortly after, her husband came home from work, when the children were playing all right, and he also started off to Framlingham. After the father left, the oldest boy relit the fire and put some wood and coal on; and carried the deceased into the backhouse and laid her before the fire. He then went out to play again.

When he went back in the house, he saw his sister was burnt to death; and as he was crying in the garden, a little girl named Sarah Kettle was passing and asked him what was the matter, when he told her. She ran to a neighbour named Burrows but when he went into the house, he found the child dead and lying about two yards from the grate of the fire, with a piece of burning wood near to her. Burrows was working in a garden nearby but did not hear the deceased scream. Verdict, "Accidental Death."

The eldest boy must have carried the memory of this shocking event into his adult life and, like many of the family witnesses to all these human tragedies, we can hardly imagine how awful those memories must have been.

Fatal Cart Accident at Debenham

In May, a fatal accident resulted in an inquest being held at the Lion Inn, Debenham before C.C. Brooke, Coroner, on the body of Charles Fairweather, aged eleven years. Deceased met with his death under the following circumstances. It appeared that on Wednesday 4th, he was carting manure with two other lads on Mr. Lock's farm, and whilst attempting to get upon the shaft of the tumbril, in order to ride, the horse kicked, in consequence of which he fell, when the wheel passed over his head and one arm, killing him instantaneously. The Jury, after viewing the body and examining the witnesses, returned a verdict of "Accidental Death."

Fatal Accident at Little Glemham

Mr. C.C. Brooke, Coroner, also visited Little Glemham for the inquest into the death of Jonathan Bridges, aged 30 years. It appeared that deceased, his father, and others were employed on the 2nd July loading clover in a field. The deceased was on the waggon loading the clover, and his father was pitching it up to him. There being a good deal of wind at the time, deceased's hat blew off over the fore horse's head, causing it to turn sharply round. Deceased's father was standing by the side of the waggon and tried to catch hold of the dutfin but missed it and the horse knocked him down and ran over him, breaking one of his ribs.

A lad by the name of Cornish saw the deceased fall from the waggon; he appeared to pitch onto his head and left arm. He was at once taken home in a cart and Mr. Cochrane, surgeon, was sent for during the evening and attended him up to the time of his death. Mr. Cochrane gave evidence that deceased died from concussion of the spine caused by a severe fall. The Jury returned a verdict of "Accidental Death."

Melancholy Case of Accidental Poisoning

The newspaper report of this case was lengthy in its detail and has been abbreviated to give the main facts of the case. The report was published on August 6th 1864 following a lengthy inquest in the village of Sibton near Peasenhall. The accidental poisoning, it said, was the result of the ignorance and carelessness of an aged woman employed as a nurse. It would not surprise the reader to learn that the 80 year old woman, a poor widow, was said to have been worn out with fatigue and unequal to the duties she had undertaken. The unfortunate victim, Mrs. Brooks, was a young woman, the wife of a farmer in the parish. She died on July 26th, two days after the poison was administered. The inquest was held two days later and the principal witness, Dr. Joseph Lay, outlined the chain of events.

"The deceased was a patient of mine, 32 years old and confined on June 29th after which she had an attack of bilious fever which lasted until July 10th. She continued in a weak state of health and also had an attack of rheumatism affecting her knee. On the morning of July 24th I attended her and found her suffering from the effects of laudanum. I had not given her any laudanum to take internally, but on the previous evening I had sent over a bottle of lotion for her knee. The lotion consisted of one ounce of laudanum, half an ounce of carbonate of potash and six ounces of water. It was sent from my surgery with directions for use tied round the neck. The directions were for the lotion to be made hot and a piece of flannel to be dipped in it to be applied round the affected knee, the whole to be wrapped in oiled silk, this to be repeated as many times as necessary for the pain in the knee. Nothing else was on the bottle except the patient's name.

"When I saw her on the 24th, she was very drowsy and I thought seriously about the case. When the lotion was sent, a bottle of medicine was also sent, as she was suffering from debility and rheumatism. The medicine was half an ounce of acetate of potash and one drop of essence of lemons. This bottle was also labelled with directions for use. Everything was plainly written. I believe that an eighth part of the lotion taken internally would be sufficient to destroy the life of a person in the position that the deceased was. The lotion was a thick brown liquid, the medicine was white and transparent."

Susan Manby, the nurse, was examined by the Coroner and Jury and said that she was a widow and 80 years of age. She could not read. She received a bottle of lotion and a bottle of medicine from Mr. Lay's but did not notice them particularly and could not speak to the colour. She slept in an adjoining room to Mrs. Brooks who asked for her medicine at five o'clock on Sunday morning and she (Mamby) went to the washstand where the bottles had been placed and poured out three-quarters of a wine glass full from what she believed to be the medicine bottle. This was the quantity that Mrs. Brooks had previously been taking. She (the nurse) did not notice the smell of the lotion. She was very tired and worn out when the bottle came and soon after went to bed. Thomas Dowsing Brooks, the husband, stated that he went to see his wife at 6 o'clock. She said she felt better but would not take any more of that mixture because it was the worst she had ever had. Mr. Brooks realised that there was something amiss and went for the doctor but when he returned his wife had lapsed into unconsciousness. On Tuesday she died.

The Jury returned a verdict of death by accidental poisoning and expressed their regret that so infirm and aged a person as Mrs. Manby should have been entrusted to act as nurse in so serious a case of illness. Susan Manby spent the remaining years of her life living with her sister Jane in Laxfield, perhaps fortunate that the workhouse system did not claim her.

Fatal Accident at Washbrook

A fatal accident occurred at Washbrook on the 12th October, to a lad named Alfred Grimes. The deceased and two or three other men were at work in a crag pit in one of Mr. Cotton's fields, called "Stubbins," filling a cart with crag when a portion of it suddenly gave way, some of it falling upon the deceased's back. The men dragged the deceased away from the crag but he could scarcely speak and was unable to stand. The deceased was taken home but he did not survive the shock. The inquest, which was held on the Friday, returned a verdict of "Accidental Death."

Unexplained Death at Wetheringsett

On Saturday 10th December, an inquest was held in the parish of Wetheringsett before F.B. Marriott Esq., Coroner, on the body of Eleanor Hipperson, aged 29. The widower of the deceased stated she was as well as usual up to last Sunday, when she caught fresh cold. She kept about until Thursday morning, between 10 and 11 o'clock, when he was called out of the house by Henry Clarke. He went as quickly as he could, and found his wife sitting, apparently dying. She was about 12 yards from the door.

He assisted her in and she sat down on a chair and died in less than a quarter of an hour. When she first sat down, she said "I must die," and never spoke afterwards. She had an enlarged throat and when she had a cold she experienced difficulty in breathing.

This evidence was corroborated by Henry Clarke and his wife, and Dr. Cuthbert said he had examined the body of deceased externally, and found the throat greatly enlarged. There was no unnatural appearance about the body, and he had not the slightest doubt but that the deceased died from natural causes. He did not think that the enlarged throat had anything to do with her death, but probably there was some disease of the heart or its large vessels, which must have caused her death. The Jury returned a verdict of "Died from natural causes."

Death from Drowning at Dallinghoo
December 1864 would have been like any other December – cold, dark evenings whereby walking along country footpaths would have been very difficult. And so it proved for Henry Keeble of Kettleburgh, a 51 year old army pensioner and formerly in the 85th Regiment. The inquest, which was held at Dallinghoo, heard that, on the Sunday afternoon, on his way from Foxhall, he called in at the Castle Inn, Bredfield at about half past five o'clock and had a pint of beer. He remained there about a quarter of an hour and on leaving said he was going home. Nothing more was seen of him alive. The following morning, a few minutes before eight, Mrs. Waters left her cottage to go and get some milk. On passing near the footbridge, a few yards from her garden gate, she saw something in the water under the bridge, which she thought was a coat. On looking more closely, she saw the bottoms of the legs and boots of a man.

Assistance was obtained and the deceased was taken out of the water. He was lying on his stomach, his mouth and entire face under the water, which was about six inches deep. His hat and stick laid on the ice close to him. Deceased was quite sober when he left the inn at Bredfield. The footbridge under which deceased was found is very narrow and the Jury considered it to be very dangerous. After a full investigation, the Jury returned a verdict of "Found Drowned" and strongly recommended that the bridge should be altered.

1865

1865 proved to be another year of mishaps, tragedies and bizarre deaths. In fact, 1865 was a microcosm of the sudden deaths that befell the population of Suffolk each year and which were probably repeated in the other counties of England. It would be fair to say that the following were the most common forms of sudden death that populated the pages of the local newspapers.

Death by Drowning
Agricultural Accidents
Children Burnt to Death
Poisonings
Suicides

We shall give examples of each on the following pages; examples that were not out of the ordinary and which would be repeated time and again in the Suffolk rural environment. We begin our final chapter with a drowning at Dunwich which occurred in the summer of 1865.

Many readers who are interested in local history might have read of the church and parish outings that took place annually which rewarded a group within the parish such as the choir singers or schoolchildren. These day outings usually involved travel by waggon, charabanc and train to seaside destinations such as Southwold and Dunwich. Such day trips were often the highlight of the year and, for many, a rare glimpse of the sea. For harm to come to one of their number must have been difficult to contemplate. The newspaper report tells the sad story.

Death by Drowning at Dunwich
On Wednesday 12th July a very large party of men, women and children passed through this place (Yoxford) from Peasenhall and Sibton in seven waggons to spend the day at Dunwich. All appeared in high spirits, anticipating a merry and pleasant day which, we lament to say, was not realised. A youth named Charles Barber, aged 17, belonging to Yoxford, with a companion, started on foot to join the pleasure seekers, and while bathing with some others was unfortunately drowned.

This sad event caused the greatest consternation and alarm among the whole party, putting a stop to all further pleasure and enjoyment. The party as they returned on their way home at night were silent and cast down. No merry faces, no cheers, it was more like a funeral procession than anything else.

On Friday, an inquest was held before B.L. Gross, Esq., Coroner, when the Jury returned a verdict in accordance with the above facts. The next day (Saturday) the corpse was followed to the grave by sorrowing friends. On Sunday, the Rev. R. Firmin preached a most impressive sermon on the melancholy event, taking his text from 1 Samuel, c 20, v 3. "And as the soul liveth, there is but a step between me and death."

Fatal Accident in a Windmill

Windmills were a hazardous environment for anyone to work in, especially if the worker was wearing loose clothing, as this incident at Claydon demonstrates. Jeremiah Burch was a master miller and one wonders how a man of experience and knowledge of working mills could suffer the fate of many throughout the 19th century.

Burch hired the mill and it was at work on a windy October Wednesday. Burch wanted to oil some part of the machinery and climbed up to the top stage in the mill to put the brake on. But the mill did not completely stop and he was in the act of oiling the neck of the mill when he suddenly discovered that he was caught and being entangled in the machinery. Another man who was with him immediately got hold of him and tried to extricate him, but just at that moment a gust of wind sent the machinery round faster and he was drawn out of his grasp, his body being crushed between the wheel and the beam. The mill was stopped and assistance sent for to extricate the poor man but he was dead and the machinery had to be reversed before his body could be got clear. At the inquest two days later, before B.L. Gross, Esq., Coroner, it was stated that the principal injury was the fracture of five or six ribs on the right side which led to the rupture of the liver and irreparable damage to the lungs and chest. The Jury returned a verdict of "Accidental Death."

Child Burnt to Death

On Tuesday 14th March, an inquest was held by C.C. Brooke, Esq., Coroner, at Great Glemham on the body of Ellen Gilbert, aged four years. From the evidence it appeared that the mother of the deceased left home on Friday morning, the 10th, to go out to work. The key of the house she gave to her elder daughter

Eliza, eight years old, and she told her to light the fire, which she usually did. On her and the deceased's return from school, Mrs. Jane Peck, a neighbour, went into the house and cautioned the deceased not to play with the fire.

Eliza went out to cut some sticks. Deceased was then sitting close to the fender with a little book in her hands. Her sister had hardly gone into the yard when deceased came running out with her clothes blazing. The flames were quickly extinguished but the deceased was so much burned that she died in a very few hours. Mr. Rendle, surgeon, Saxmundham, was sent for and attended and gave evidence at the inquest as to the cause of death. The Jury immediately returned a verdict of "Death from being accidentally burned."

Death from Eating Fungus
When we think of death from poisoning in Queen Victoria's reign, we might immediately think of arsenic, used to rid habitations of vermin and which was often stored in a pantry and mistaken for flour. But there were toxic hazards elsewhere.

On Tuesday 1st August an inquest heard of the circumstances surrounding the death of Elizabeth Edwards, a girl 5 years old. The evidence went on to show that on the previous Saturday the mother had gathered from near the root of a tree what she thought to be mushrooms. She took them home and fried them and she and her daughters partook of the meal, the deceased eating rather more than the others. On Sunday they were all ill and the illness increased, especially in the deceased, who died the next day (Monday).

They were attended by a medical gentleman and the mother and other child are nearly recovered. What they had eaten was fungus, a plant very like a mushroom. The Jury returned a verdict accordingly. The Coroner sent portions of the fungus to Professor Taylor, the celebrated toxicologist who wrote back the following:

"Your letter furnishes another illustration of the sad ignorance which exists among the poor with reference to mushrooms. I have examined the substance which you have sent me and find it to be one of the poisonous kind of mushrooms, the amanita citrina, so called from the lemon-yellow colour of the cap. You ask me for a rule for distinguishing between noxious and wholesome fungi. There is only one that is wholesome and that not always or to all persons. This is the common edible mushroom – agaricus campestris." The professor then went on to explain the distinguishing features of the edible mushroom compared to poisonous fungi, information not available to the labouring poor.

Suicide and Sudden Death at Boxford
On Friday 29th September, two inquests were held at Boxford before G.A. Partridge, Esq., Coroner. The first concerned the body of Thomas Elmer a brickmaking labourer, aged 42 years, who fatally shot himself in the head. On Wednesday morning, after rising early to assist his master, who was going to London by the excursion train from Sudbury, deceased told his wife that he would get his gun and shoot a rabbit. He seemed in his usual spirits and went to the brickfields and smoked a pipe He then went into the backhouse and shortly afterwards his wife heard the report of a gun and found her husband lying on the floor quite dead. He had tied a piece of string to the trigger and pulled

it with his foot whilst holding the gun to his head. His head was completely shattered and his brains bespattered the ceiling.

Mr. T.G. Gurdon, surgeon, said that the deceased was very hypochondrical and often complained of his throat, chest and head, but his ailments were more imaginary than anything else. His mind was much distressed at times and he suffered from want of sleep. The Jury returned a verdict in line with the evidence of Elmer's unsound state of mind.

Immediately after the first inquest, the body of Mary Wright, a widow, aged 67 years, was brought in and laid out for the Jury. It transpired that on Wednesday morning, deceased went to the house of a friend by the name of Munson and asked her if she had heard of Elmer having destroyed himself. She walked home and returned to Mrs. Munson's house at about 20 minutes past 11; about half an hour afterwards, she suddenly exclaimed "Oh Dear!" and fell off the chair, on which she was sitting, only breathing once after she was picked up. Mr. C.P. Mann, surgeon, had no doubt that death arose from natural causes – apoplexy, he should say. Verdict, "Natural Death."

No mention of it being "Death by the Visitation of God."

And so we conclude our journey amongst the ranks of the dear departed who suffered misery and misfortune before being memorialised in the inquest records and newspaper reports of the distant past.

APPENDICES

LIST OF PARISHES
The parishes in which the inquests in this book took place are listed here alphabetically.

Alderton, Ashfield-cum-Thorpe, Bardwell, Bawdsey, Bedfield, Benhall, Blaxhall, Boxford, Bramfield, Brandeston, Bredfield, Brent Eleigh, Brockford, Brome, Bromeswell, Brundish, Bungay, Burgate, Bury St. Edmunds, Butley, Buxhall, Campsey Ashe, Carlton Colville, Charsfield, Chelmondiston, Clare, Claydon, Clopton, Coddenham, Combs, Cookley, Creeting St. Mary, Dallinghoo, Debenham, Dennington, Drinkstone, Earl Soham, Earl Stonham, East Bergholt, Eriswell, Eye, Farnham, Finningham, Framlingham, Framsden, Fressingfield, Friston, Gazeley, Gislingham, Great Bealings, Great Finborough, Great Glemham, Grundisburgh, Halesworth, Harkstead, Hawstead, Helmingham, Heveningham, Hintlesham, Holbrook, Horham, Hundon, Ilketshall St. Andrew, Ipswich, Kedington, Kessingland, Kettleburgh, Lavenham, Lawshall, Laxfield, Little Glemham, Little Thurlow, Long Melford, Lowestoft, Melton, Mendham, Mendlesham, Mildenhall, Needham Market, Occold, Offton, Oulton, Ousden, Parham, Peasenhall, Rishangles, Rumburgh, Saxtead, Sibton, Snape, Somerleyton, Somersham, Southwold, Spexhall, Stanstead, Sternfield, Stowmarket, Stradbroke, Stratford St. Andrew, Sudbourne, Sudbury, Sutton, Sweffling, Tannington, Thorndon, Thornham Magna, Thurston, Troston, Tuddenham, Waldringfield, Wangford, Washbrook, Wenhaston, Wetheringsett, Weybread, Wherstead, Wickham Market, Wickham Skeith, Wilby, Winston, Wissett, Witnesham, Woodbridge, Woolpit, Worlingworth, Wrentham, Yaxley, Yoxford.

LIST OF SURNAMES

Ager	Edwards	Kent	Rolfe
Aldous	Ellis	Kerridge	Rose
Aldridge	Emeny	King	Rudd
Baldry	Emmerson	Kistruck	Ruddock
Barber	Evans	Knights	Rush
Barham	Everitt	Lambert	Sadd
Barker	Fairweather	Lancaster	Sawyer
Barwell	Farrow	Last	Scates
Betts	Flatt	Leeder	Seammen
Bigsby	French	Leggatt	Searle
Birch	Fuller	Levett	Sherman
Bloomfield	Garrod	Ling	Ship
Bloss	Gathercole	Long	Short
Boast	Gilbert	Mabson	Simpson
Boon	Gladding	Macon	Skoulding
Bootman	Gladwell	Mann	Smith
Brewington	Goddard	Markham	Sones
Bridges	Golby	Marjoram	Symonds
Briggs	Goldsmith	Martin	Taylor
Brooks	Good	Meadows	Thurman
Brown	Gough	Mingay	Thurston
Brunning	Green	Moor	Tillett
Buck	Grice	Murrell	Tissington
Buckle	Grimes	Mutimer	Turtill
Bull	Grimwood	Newby	Tye
Burch	Hall	Nunn	Vale
Burrowes	Hamby	Osbourne	Wade
Burrows	Hammond	Page	Watling
Catchpole	Harvey	Paramore	Watson
Cattermole	Hawkes	Pearson	Wells
Chatten	Hewitt	Peck	White
Chester	Hipperson	Pipe	Whiterod
Church	Hughes	Pooley	Whitmore
Cleveland	Hugman	Potkin	Woods
Cole	Hunt	Powling	Woodward
Cooper	Hurren	Pryke	Woolnough
Copping	Jarvis	Radford	Young
Cornwell	Jay	Ranson	
Dale	Jolly	Ray	
Denny	Joslyn	Reynolds	
Dykes	Keeble	Riches	